THE MYSTERIOUS FORCES

G S Vaid

MINERVA PRESS
NEW DELHI
MIAMI LONDON

THE MYSTERIOUS FORCES

ISBN 81 7662 144 7

First Published 2001 by
MINERVA PRESS
13 Palam Marg
Vasant Vihar
New Delhi – 110 057

Printed & bound in India
for Minerva Press (India) Pvt. Ltd.

THE MYSTERIOUS FORCES

I humbly request my esteemed readers
to kindly ignore my lack of command of the language
and deficient expressions here and there
as I am neither semantically gifted,
nor a professional writer.

Despite these shortcomings,
I have simply, but honestly, tried
to convey to my readers the outcome (inferences), of my
experiments relating to the verdicts (reactions), of
the all-pervading, omniscient, celestial forces,
to the karmas (actions), of the embodied souls
that I have monitored closely.

The contents of this book
may not be found suitable
for those who are too materialistic to hear their Inner Voice
—The Voice of the Soul.

The incidents predicted
in this book are true, to the best
of my observations and close monitoring.

Dedicated to those rare souls who,
with their Inner Eyes, can see a flawless justification
behind each and every act of
the all-pervading, omniscient, marvellous
but invisible celestial forces, governing the universe.

My obeisance to those amiable, subtle
embodied souls, who are mentally and spiritually
not present in the elusive activities of the world.

My special thanks to
Mr Vinod Dhawan
for the valuable assistance rendered
by him in bringing out this book.

Chapter I

There are in this universe; unique forces in existence beyond the comprehension of human beings at large. These are perennial, all-pervading, all-powerful, omniscient, divinely subtle and in complete control of the universe in its entirety. We may, in simple words, call these as the mysterious forces governing the universe under His supreme command.

These are our Creator's creation and have been in existence ever since the beginning of this world. Obviously, these have no beginning and are endless.

These celestial forces completely control the physical and mental activities of all the embodied souls. Their functioning is celestially flawless, automatic, methodical, vindictive, immaculate, but certainly beyond the understanding of most of us.

An average human being, probably, is sceptical of the existence of any such force. Most people are simply not prepared to believe that their earthly existence is strictly monitored and controlled by these natural forces. They feel they are free to do anything they like, unhindered and unchecked and claim to be the 'masters of their wills'.

'Man is born free but everywhere he is in chains,' has very rightly been said by someone.

Here, the chains in fact, are symbolic restrictions and checks imposed by the forces, on the physical and mental activities of the embodied souls.

All living beings of course, have been bestowed with a little freedom of will. But this does not mean that one is free to go to any extent, or overstep the ultimate natural barriers. One can't afford to go beyond one's parameters. The natural barriers are like *lakshman rekhas* (the fire-emitting lines), and whosoever tries to overstep these, gets burnt, which (in other words), means he gets physical or mental punishment in commensuration with his violation of natural rules. Nature's laws are so rigid and authentic that no living being on earth can violate them unharmed.

People, deluded by earthly activities (i.e. materialism and physical comforts), often try to overstep their lakshman rekhas and in turn, go on inviting troubles and ultimately become the major source of their mental and physical sufferings.

The marvellous but mysterious forces react commensurately to the bad and good karmas (actions) of the embodied souls. At the same time, these subtle forces undoubtedly, protect the really virtuous people perennially in unique ways, probably beyond the comprehension of an ordinary being.

I have keenly observed in a number of cases how the forces protect some people in immaculately planned but unique ways – ways, which perhaps, can't be explained perfectly in words.

However, I have tried to depict the working of the forces with the help of a number of episodes which are true and based on the happenings and incidents occurring around me at different times, in mysterious ways.

Each happening around me strengthened my belief in the existence of the all-pervading, unique forces – of course, invisible to the human eyes of the embodied soul.

In fact, each and every living being in this world, remains perennially surrounded by the forces which keep on rewarding or punishing the individual, depending upon his moment-to-moment karmas.

I was once travelling in an arduous mountainous terrain,

in one of Nepal's remotest regions, between two sleepy hamlets, about seventeen kilometres apart, in a small-bodied truck, in the company of two others. We commenced the journey around two o'clock when the weather appeared to be favourable for undertaking the journey. The sky was quite clear.

Soon our truck was zigzagging on an unmetalled, undulated, narrow road, passing through lush green hills and valleys. It was dangerously negotiating sharp curves and blind turnings. The driver however, appeared to be very alert and was driving the truck very cautiously, on this extremely bad road surface.

Hardly had we covered about half the distance when thick clouds started appearing in the sky, from all directions. Soon we found ourselves caught in a furious, high-velocity storm, accompanied by a heavy downpour, lasting well over an hour. The driver had brought the truck to a screeching halt seconds before the beginning of the heavy downpour. The road had become slippery and slushy.

As the rain stopped, we got down from the truck to assess the condition of the road. All of us, including the driver, were of the opinion that the road surface ahead was far from satisfactory and as such, decided to wait for some time. The driver however, appeared to be very interested in reaching our destination well before sunset.

We waited for an hour or so and then decided to move. The truck started but could not pick up speed because the road surface was still slippery. It kept on moving for some distance at an extremely slow speed. The driver seemed to be overcautious while negotiating the sharp, dangerous curves and abrupt turnings, in order to avoid skidding at any cost. And now it was, by and large, a straight, levelled stretch before us. The driver increased the speed a little. We felt somewhat relieved of our mental stress and strain.

Suddenly, there was a thunderous sound and in no time,

we were stunned to see a huge chunk of the hill sliding down the road. Our truck thus came to a screeching halt once again. In the meantime, it started raining again, but as a drizzle this time. In the minutes that followed, we saw the full width of the road covered with the landslide debris.

Spotting a truck and a covered jeep coming from the opposite direction and gradually stopping on the other side of the road—blockage, our driver decided to move and get close to the landslide site, to assess whether a part of the road width could be cleared, with the joint efforts of all.

As we were nearing the road-blockage, our truck started skidding towards the valley. Instantly, the driver shouted for a 'quick jump'. We all jumped out of the truck with our small belongings, without the loss of a moment.

In the ensuing moments, we saw our truck rolling down the deep ravine. We had undoubtedly, a miraculous escape from the jaws of certain death.

I was too stunned to react to what had suddenly happened in a few moments' time. None of us had received any major injury. I was the only one who had escaped completely unhurt, without even a minor scratch on any part of my body. We all thanked Him for sparing our lives.

I attributed this miraculous escape from the jaws of death to a quirk of fate, meticulously engineered by the all-pervading, omniscient, omnipotent, mysterious forces, that govern the universe under His supreme command and control.

I shall now be delineating another true incident attributable to a quirk of fate.

A major train accident, involving an express train and a passenger train, took place in the wee hours of New Year's Day, 1958, at a small railway station called Mohri, near Ambala, resulting in heavy loss of life.

'Human error' was reported to be the cause of the accident and later was established as such, by the investigating experts. What happened on that fateful day goes like this:

A passenger train was detained at Mohri station as an express train was to bypass it. During those days, the Delhi-Ambala section used to be single-tracked. As such, the not-so-important trains (such as ordinary passenger trains, shuttles, goods trains), used to be detained or made to wait, sometimes for hours, simply to allow the express and mail trains to cross them.

The accident at Mohri, I distinctly remember, had been attributed to carelessness and negligence on the part of the pointsman (who, it was said, died of sudden shock the very moment the trains collided). The cries of the badly injured and the survivors, trapped in the bogies, rent the air. Some nearby villagers swung into action and saved many lives. Later, official rescue teams joined them and started the rescue operation on a war footing. Besides the seriously injured, the death casualty was stated to be in the hundreds. At least nine bogies and the engines (locomotives), of both the trains were a complete wreck.

One of my distant relatives, in his early sixties at that time, happened to be travelling in the ill-fated passenger train. It was the wee hours of one of the coldest wintry days and as such, most of the passengers were still asleep, blanket-clad.

To overcome his boredom, my relative got off his coach and started strolling on the platform, also looking for a cup of tea. Finding no tea vendor on the platform, he headed towards the station exit to explore the possibility of a tea-vending kiosk (khoka etc.), outside the station. The moment he stepped out of the exit, he heard a thunderous, deafening sound behind. As he looked back to see what had happened, he was shocked to see the horrible collision of the trains. He became motionless when he saw that the compartment he had been in, a few moments earlier, had collapsed into a heap of junk.

According to my relative, not a single occupant of that compartment had survived.

Obviously that man, the only survivor of the ill-fated compartment, escaped completely unhurt, by a quirk of fate caused by the celestial forces, the functions of which are mysterious and beyond a common man's comprehension.

It was the all-pervading, omnipotent, divine forces which took the man away from his compartment, to a safe distance, moments before the collision of the trains, on the pretext of his boredom and the desire for a cup of tea.

Thus we see how these gracious forces at times make their presence felt, by singling out and saving someone, in a unique and mysterious way.

Chapter II

There are human beings (rare, of course), who are bestowed with inner eyes with which they can distinctly see these marvellous forces at work. These *third-eyed,* embodied souls, do know in the real sense that there is always a flawless justification behind each and every act (function), of the forces. They are spiritually capable of understanding that they are accountable to these all-powerful forces for each and every act of theirs – physical as well as mental.

They know they shall be receiving punishment at the hands of the forces, sooner or later, for their bad karmas. They thus keep themselves aloof from the vices of the world. They do not indulge in malignant activities or embrace corrupt means for their livelihood, or for physical comforts, in their lifetime. Obviously, this category of people, the world over, are harmless creatures of the Creator.

On the other hand, the commoners hardly believe in the existence of such forces. They obviously, are sceptical of their presence in any shape or form. Thus, ignoring them (the forces), they keep themselves engaged in materialism throughout their lives, with the sole aim of acquiring more and more assets and physical comforts, by fair means or foul.

They don't mind accumulating wealth at the cost of their fellow beings, by squeezing their blood. They remain unconcerned towards the harm they do to the society at large and care only for their own bread and butter. Obviously, such people do not believe that they will be punished for their malignant acts in any way, by any force or power on earth.

Such disillusioned, heartless souls, cannot get at one of nature's cardinal laws of 'perpetually keeping the equilibrium between crime and punishment, by the omnipotent forces'. These diabolic people undoubtedly remain losers in innumerable ways (beyond a commoner's understanding), though they may appear to be outwardly flourishing or prospering, in the likeness of an optical illusion. The forces punish a man commensurably for his offences. There is no escape. The forces, of course, take their own time in meting out punishment to the offenders, but certainly no offender can get away unharmed, or scot-free. Sometimes, the offender is punished instantly. The forces switch into action and start their work the moment an offender commits an offence. The offender may run away and hide himself, at a place he considers safe, after committing the crime, but the forces continue to chase him in mysterious ways till he is completely cornered.

It is not true that virtuous and noble souls do not suffer. They, too, suffer from time to time, from physical and mental disabilities. Our mortal world is a blend of joys and sorrows and there are more sorrows than joys as per nature's thumb-rule. However, the sufferings of really virtuous souls are not comparable with those of evildoers, or people with negative traits.

An evildoer's sufferings are, by and large, of a perennial nature, while a noble man's sufferings are of a non-perennial nature, lasting for short durations. But the sufferings are there – both for evildoers and the noble ones. There are, by nature, always more sufferings in store for the evildoers. They, in fact, never remain at peace, by and large, throughout their lifespan, while the amiable and virtuous ones remain unperturbed under all circumstances. Hence they lead a peaceful life, despite many odds. The noble souls are bound to come out victorious in the last run, while the evil ones go to complete ruin, some day.

The gracious forces perpetually protect the noble people from time to time, from the onslaughts of evildoers. These marvellous, celestial forces, come to the rescue of the pure, virtuous souls, at the time of their need. Here, I am talking of really virtuous embodied souls and certainly not of hypocrites.

Coming back to the forces—these invisible (to the eye), but all-powerful, subtle, gracious forces, are friendly to those who are simple-hearted, pious, virtuous, compassionate to all living beings, amiable, inwardly and outwardly pure, logical in their talks, temperament and acts and preachers of universal brotherhood and peace. These gracious forces always stand by noble-embodied souls and guard them against worldly troubles. They sometimes drastically make their presence felt, in seemingly fragile, ordinary, embodied souls.

Many a time proud and physically strong men, full of vanity, can be seen getting defeated at the hands of ordinary, freak and weak persons, in inexplicable, miraculous ways.

Off The Track

Do you avoid the crowd around you or does the crowd avoid you?

In the first case, you surely are a peace-loving, harmless guy. And in the second case, you most probably are a hypocrite.

Chapter III

I was in Nepal for a little over four years in the late seventies and early eighties, in connection with the execution of a prestigious highway project, that aimed at providing an approximately 160 kilometre long, all-weather road link, between the eastern and western regions of Nepal.

The proposed alignment of the highway passed through a semi-hilly area, with dense forests and was infested with wildlife. The entire alignment passed through one of the remotest regions of Nepal.

The technical, as well as non-technical staff, engaged on this project were accommodated in temporary camps, scattered on the proposed alignment, at an average distance of about thirteen kilometres from one another. Each camp comprised of about six, temporary dwelling units, one office, a store and a hutment for workers, such as drivers, operators, mechanics etc. By and large, all the camps existed on a high land (hillocks etc.), just by the side of the alignment, surrounded by wildlife infested forests, hills and meadows. We had been working under minimum, basic facilities. We used to be virtually cut off from the rest of the world during the monsoon period, which lasted about five months every year. The project, however, was full of challenges, and exhilarating, too.

I was stationed at a camp situated at the mid-point of the road alignment, close to a small, sleepy hamlet. Being engineers, our field duty was extremely hard and to keep our spirits and morale high, as well as to overcome our day's fatigue, we used to assemble at a common venue of course, within the camp precincts, in the evening, for a drink and a chit-chat. Besides, we used to play indoor-games, narrate personal experiences of interest to each other and offer prayers to the Almighty. All the members of the camp used to stroll within the camp limits, after having their dinner, before finally retiring to their beds.

Once (I think it was in November, 1980), a badminton tournament was organised at our camp, in which about fourteen participants from four camps were to take part. Much against my wishes, I was also made to participate in the tournament, as I had never been a badminton player in my life hitherto. I did not even know the basic rules of the game. Anyhow, I was acquainted with the rules by my camp colleagues a few days in advance of the date of commencement of the tournament. However, I was not given any coaching by anybody. I started practising – half-heartedly of course, by playing friendly matches with a few of my colleagues.

The tournament days approached. In all, twenty-six matches, including quarter-finals, semi-finals and finals, were played. I was made to face twelve 'singles' in all.

Some of my colleagues I was to face had been champions of this game in their school and college days and were also younger than I, by several years. Despite all these odds, I played all the ties absolutely anxiety-free, but certainly with my full stamina. And, to my surprise, I did not lose a single match. All the participants were simply astonished at my outstanding performance. They called it a miracle. I was declared the unbeaten champion of the tournament!

Truly speaking, my outstanding performance kept haunting me for many days. So many questions struck my mind—How did it happen? How was I so full of energy during the match hours? What was the source of my energy? How was it possible for me to remain unbeaten at the hands of those who had been the champions of their school and college days? Ultimately I got the answers to my questions, as expressed in these words, 'The invisible but all-powerful gracious natural forces, at times, drastically and amazingly make their presence felt, in seemingly ordinary, fragile embodied souls. We simply call such inexplicable happenings miracles.

My older daughter had been just average at her studies, right from Standard One to her graduation, unlike her younger sister. Both the girls received their education in a public school of repute, upto class twelve under the 'ten-plus-two' system and then both did their graduation from Delhi University.

The elder of the two had been an extraordinarily loveable child, because of some of her extraordinarily fine traits. She was simple, soft-spoken, straightforward, innocent-looking, fair-complexioned, cute, compassionate, amiable and above all, an absolutely harmless creature of the Almighty.

Despite her poor performance in some of her subjects, in her House tests and final exams, she continued to remain the darling of her class teachers, as well as many of her classmates.

I often used to be summoned by her school principal (a high-profile, foreign lady), to explain to her, in person, the causes of her 'not up to the mark' performance in examinations and periodic tests. Every time I would feel embarrassed while face-to-face with the principal. It used to be awfully difficult for me, at times, to face the volley of question and every time I would assure her of a better performance, 'next time'.

It would not be out of place to mention that my close study and monitoring of this daughter of mine, often made me to ponder over her amazing expressions (at times) and her spiritual disposition, when she was in her teens.

To me, she appeared to be very close to nature in many

respects. She seemed to carry an old head on her young shoulders. According to her teachers, she was conspicuously different from her classmates in many ways. Most of her classmates came from rich homes, but she, I am sure, never felt jealous of their riches and privileges. She never uttered a single, indecent word, or used abusive or hurtful language for anybody around her.

Once, her class teacher asked her to bring a thousand rupees as a contribution towards bringing out a special souvenir by the school, on its Annual-Day celebrations. Her straightforward but polite reply to her teacher was, 'Ma'am, I am sorry, I won't be able to contribute one thousand rupees, as my father does not have any black money with him. He just can't afford it.' Her class teacher was simply taken aback by this bold reply by my daughter. However, her teacher did not mind all this, according to my daughter.

My daughter never felt small telling her friends (class, schoolmates etc.), that her father was financially not sound enough to provide her facilities and the basic comforts, unlike theirs. She also used to tell them that she was proud of her father, because of his extraordinarily good nature and positive traits.

I distinctly remember she could expound convincingly the workings of nature under His scheme of things, when she was in her eighth standard.

Her utterances sometimes, used to be 'saint-like'. She seldom showed interest in visiting places of worship or attending religious gatherings as she considered, 'the human body itself a temple of the living God'. Besides, she possessed an amazing intuitive power. She was a reserved child, who did not like to mix with hypocritical crowds, although she had an excellent sense of humour too. She was and still is, a great lover of music, songs of the fifties and sixties and pop music, which she listens to, in her spare time.

She once abruptly told her mother that she often had visions of flying high in the air, at a terrific speed. During her first year at college, she contested for the 'best model of the college' and was pronounced the 'best model' by a jury of Japanese, high-profile ladies. She completed her graduation, by and large, with qualifying marks. But her dream of flying high in the air really came true.

A day in her early twenties saw her flying high in the sky, at a terrific speed, in an aircraft, as a highly successful air hostess.

Even years after becoming an air hostess, she continued to remain reserved, showing little interest in visiting crowded places. But her natural instinct of visiting nature-blessed panoramas never vanished. I call her a happy-go-lucky creature of Divine Nature.

She was not a privileged child, unlike her rich friends, during her many, education-receiving years. But a time came when she found herself bestowed with all the amenities and necessities of 'high profile' (comfortable), living by the grace of the omnipotent, omniscient, divine forces.

This real story clearly suggests that the all-powerful, gracious forces, perpetually take care of the amiable children of God and carry them to comfortable positions from humble ones, in course of time, in unique ways.

Off The Track

The easiest task on earth is to criticise, while the toughest task is to face criticism.

Chapter IV

I had been, by and, large, an average student, throughout my education-receiving period. In 1958, I was in the first year of my Civil Engineering course. During those days, clearing one paper of Mechanical Engineering and one of Electrical Engineering, along with the first year's annual examination, used to be mandatory for all the Civil Engineering students. Similar was the case of Mechanical and Electrical Engineering students. In fact, the first year of all the branches of Engineering used to be common, for all the Engineering students.

I was made to join Civil Engineering against my will. It was on the insistence of my parents, who wanted me to be an engineer that I had joined the course. Immediately after joining the polytechnic, I found myself uneasy with Mechanical Engineering. My immediate reaction was to get myself withdrawn, as qualifying the mandatory paper in Mechanical Engineering appeared to me to be an uphill task. At the same time, I was also deeply concerned with the sentiments of my parents who wanted to see me an engineer. At one stage I thought I would never be able to clear the Mechanical paper, but somehow, I was supposed to clear it, for completing my engineering. Considering all these things, I gradually started compromising with my circumstances and started devoting the maximum possible time to the Mechanical. Then, because of my strong will power, I became resolute about overcoming my weakness and determined to clear this paper. I laboured hard and succeeded in preparing my own notes, with the utmost care with the help of text books, books on the subject available in the library of the polytechnic and class notes. The days rolled by swiftly and the annual examination days seemed to be approaching at a fast pace. By this time, I had succeeded in building self-confidence in myself, to a considerable extent. But still, I felt my fear of clearing the Mechanical paper had not yet evaporated.

The day came on which the Mechanical Engineering paper was to be held. The question paper had been distributed and I found myself concentrating on its contents. I overpowered my anxiety and thought of tackling those questions first, which I felt I had prepared well.

I still distinctly remember that one of the questions (carrying the maximum marks), was on the practical functioning (and working) of an I.C.E. (Internal Combustion Engine). On the whole, this question was considered comparatively tougher and I knew that most of my Engineering classmates were awfully afraid of it. I completed the I.C.E. question with the help of about ten sketches, depicting the position of the I.C.E. in every one-tenth of a second. No text book dealing with I.C.E. contained more than two or three figures. Finishing the I.C.E. question to my utmost satisfaction, boosted my morale. Then I found myself handling the rest of the questions on a war footing. I was in a position to finish all the questions by the stipulated time, to my utmost satisfaction.

The examination was over in about ten days and I became sure I had fared well in all the papers.

The result came after a wait of a little over two months. I was simply stunned to find myself at position one, in the Mechanical Engineering paper, securing eighty-nine per cent marks, against an overall percentage of sixty-eight (in the aggregate). Later, I was told I had topped the Board in the Mechanical Engineering paper and was advised to switch over to Mechanical Engineering. Truly speaking, I never thought I would top the paper I was so terribly afraid of it. Frankly, I had never been above average at my studies, right from standard one, to the finish.

Ridiculously, my service period (of my profession, spanning nearly three-and-a-half decades), saw me, at times, excelling over my superiors, in a number of respects. The concluding four years of my service period brought me into the limelight, as a highly successful organiser of national level symposiums.

Such amazing happenings, from time to time, made me believe staunchly in the existence of an all-pervading, omniscient, gracious, but invisible, mysterious force which, at times, make their presence felt in a humble ordinary embodied soul, in countless unique ways.

For decades I had been, as a student and as a professional, carrying out experiments in the spiritual laboratory, housed in my body and soul, on the basis of the behaviour of human beings (who remained in close touch with me for many years and even decades in some cases), towards the supreme powers. Some of my close kin and acquaintances became indispensable equipment and ingredients of my unique lab. I monitored (of course wittily, at times), their actions (the good as well as the bad ones), and also monitored how the omnipotent, celestial forces, reacted to their karmas, sooner or later.

Chapter V

A celebrated scientist of his time, Newton, gave this world a number of scientific laws on forces which have remained and will continue to remain evergreen and ever true.

One of his laws says, 'To every action, there is an equal and opposite reaction.' In simple words, we may interpret this as 'Actions and reactions are equal and opposite.'

In order to prove the authenticity of his law, Newton put forth a number of convincing examples. He says, 'If you strike a ball against the wall, it will come back to you with the same force with which it was struck against the wall.' This example is apparently synonymous with the universally acknowledged basic principle of life, according to which, as you will sow, so shall you reap.

Newton certainly was nature's great gift to the world of science. To me, he was a born scientist who possessed inner eyes with which he could visualise nature's mysterious but invisible forces at work. He was a celestially blessed mortal who had descended on earth to explore the secrets of nature. And that is why his scientific discoveries (laws), truly resemble natural phenomena without the slightest doubt.

For example, Newton's Law of Actions and Reactions and Divine Nature's maintaining the equilibrium of 'reactions' to an individual's 'actions', are clearly one and the same thing. These two phenomena are synonymous. Man acts and nature reacts commensurately. Similarly, the balance of crime and punishment is flawlessly and perennially kept, by the omnipotent forces. There is a punishment for one in commensuration with the crime one commits at any given time. No one can escape this.

The maxim, 'Do good and have good,' is symbolic of the basic principle of life which is, as you sow, so shall you reap. That means, one is bound to get the reactions of one's good or bad actions.

We thus come to the conclusion (if we all sincerely acknowledge it), that Newton's Law of forces, the basic principle of life and the universally acknowledged maxim (Do good and have good)—all convey to human beings one and the same message.

These three phenomena are synonymous with one another.

The truth that remains perennially, is thus—An embodied soul is immaculately accountable to the omnipotent, mysterious forces, for all its karmas (actions).

Chapter VI

The journey of all living entities, from attachment (sheer ignorance), to liberation (eternal bliss), is long, tedious, extremely painful, devoid of tranquillity, restless and spanning many births. Most human beings, deluded by the physical glitter of the world, fail to get themselves extricated from the non-stop shackle of births and deaths. The wise on the other hand, are those who constantly meditate (with an undivided mind), over the cycle of birth and death—the blemishes and sorrows of their physical existence, by shunning ignorance and embracing Real Knowledge, and by doing so, they gradually succeed in getting close to His scheme of things. Soon they get purified and become amiable and get at the Right Path, leading them finally to eternal bliss.

Then there are those who, out of sheer ignorance (lack of real knowledge), keep on embracing the fascinating materialism of the world that ultimately leads them to the point of no return. And yet there are others who, deluded by too much materialism, destroy themselves to the depths of hell and thus remain suspended in the unending cycle of birth and death, that is extremely painful. The wise men, on the other hand, long for liberation from their physical existence as they truly know that taking birth and dying is extremely painful. The foolish, love the attachments of the deluding physical existence. They do not shun attachments, come what may. They do not believe in the natural phenomenon of painful births and deaths and apparently long for a physical existence only.

It depends upon the individual as to how much time he

needs to come out of the cycle of births and deaths and attain eternity. Some rare persons can attain it in a single birth, while most human beings fail to reach the grand finale even in their innumerable births. The fact is that the moment an embodied soul succeeds in touching a specific inexplicable, spiritual level (perfection), it becomes eligible for eternity—Liberation from the cycle of birth and death.

And yet, there are even those (rarest of the rare of course), who lead sinful lives, yet succeed in heading towards perfection at breakneck speed, at any given time, with the blessings of the supernatural powers (the mysterious forces), and ultimately attain their goal (liberation from physical existence).

Committing an offence against His creatures amounts to waging a war against Him. Whenever one commits an offence or a heinous crime merely for one's material gains and nothing goes wrong with one for quite some time, one should not think one has escaped punishment at the hands of the omnipotent forces, and that one has gone scot-free. It should be taken for granted that one is bound to be punished, sooner or later, for one's offence. There is, absolutely no doubt about this.

All living beings have in store for them sufferings as well as blissful spells. A universally acknowledged fact is that there are more sufferings than joys, for all of us in this mortal world. Human beings at large perpetually remain surrounded by physical and mental problems. Of course there are some heavenly-blessed, embodied souls, who do not let the problems and worldly ills override them. They, by and large, remain unperturbed under all circumstances. They keep themselves above physical joys and sorrows.

The cycle of surfacing and vanishing and resurfacing and revanishing of worldly ills (physical and mental miseries), is everlasting. There is no escape for anyone. Exceptions do not prove the rule.

Chapter VII

I can, with my limited inner vision, see the gracious natural forces functioning flawlessly, in league with amiable, embodied souls.

My obeisance is to these pure and enlightened souls who are mentally (spiritually), not present in the superficial activities of the world. I adore them, like I adore my creator. To me, they are no smaller than my God.

On the other hand, there are those who have been embracing the demoniac forces of nature. They are the destroyers of the world peace. All the worldly vices and destruction emanate from them. Hatchers of heinous crime, such as abductors, saboteurs, extortionists, dacoits, robbers, bomb exploders, cold-blooded killers, intruders etc.—all belong to this category of people.

And then there are persons who are a blend of good and bad, virtues and vices. These people, in their actions, are neither too good, nor too bad. They are, undoubtedly materialistic, but a little God-fearing too. They are born not to deliver much good to mankind. At the same time, they are not completely spiritually dead, either.

There is yet another category of people who have in them more virtues than vices. They possess more positive traits than negative ones. They certainly are not of much menace to the world. They are social and helpful to their fellow beings. However, because of some of their negative traits, they at times ignore their fellow beings for their own advantage and physical comforts, but they are surely not so harmful to His creatures. This category of people, by and large, make up about half of the human race.

They are, more or less, peace-loving, God-fearing, compassionate and considerate.

Last of all, there are people who possess more vices than virtues. Their negative traits override their positive ones. People in this category embrace selfishness and staunchly believe in amassing wealth, by hook or by crook. They can go to any extent in deceiving their fellow beings simply for their personal gains and comforts. They clearly are opportunists, impostors, and hypocrites, who constantly remain interested in their own selves. Such people are harmful to the society at large. They are least bothered if their nation, or the world, goes to pieces. They are trouble-creators in many respects, while they claim they are social caretakers of the downtrodden. The hard fact, however, remains that they are no better than bloodsuckers. They are like termites, perennially eating away world prosperity, for their selfish gains and material comforts. They are cheats by all standards, but they call themselves the servants of the people of the Almighty.

Shrewd and corrupt public figures (politicians), their henchmen, self-styled godmen, trade union leaders, most social workers, office bearers of political parties, fundamentalists, most clergymen, fanatics, heads of most of the political parties, most of the religious heads, blackmarketeers, most of our ministers, chief ministers, high-ups in ministries, the fuss-creators, trouble-makers (at the slightest pretext), most of the men in authority—etc.—all belong to this category of the human race. Although their percentage is not high, yet they rule over the world, in one way or another.

They are first-class deceivers and impostors and great exploiters of situations to their own advantage. The irony is that people at large, the world over, cannot get rid of these demons—the destroyers of the social fabric of society. They violate all man-made and nature-made norms and continue to remain fearless in their bad karmas, so long as they do not get cornered by the all-pervading, omnipotent natural forces.

These people have often been seen to be suffering intensely in innumerable ways, particularly, in the concluding days of their lives. A stage comes in their lives (sooner or later), when they start feeling that their lives have become meaningless and no longer worth living. This, in fact, is the stage at which these bad people start feeling the presence of the omnipotent forces that are capable of overriding them for their wrongdoing and misadventures. Then they feel they are undone and cannot get out of the grip of the forces—which ultimately makes them realise the natural phenomenon of crime versus punishment. In their later days they suffer immensely, from innumerable physical ailments and mental problems, as a consequence of which they no longer remain interested in living any more. Needless to mention, people in this category never remain at peace and meet with tragic ends, in the last run.

At the same time it has been observed that really sincere leaders, with patriotism in their blood, have lived long in peace. Their number, no doubt, is very small. Where there are corrupt leaders, there are dedicated ones also, to counter them. Unfortunately, in today's political scene, the patriots have been overshadowed by the corrupt. However, one thing is very certain; the time is not far off when the mysterious, omnipotent forces will come to the rescue of sincere leaders and a new, altogether changed political scene, will emerge mysteriously, eclipsing the corrupt.

There is no dearth of godmen—not only in India but the world over, particularly in south Asia. And there is no dearth of followers of these self-styled godmen. The so-called godmen—generally in saffron or yellow robes, wearing *rudraksh maalas* and rosaries and displaying a huge but fascinating tilak on the forehead, can be seen mesmerising their followers with their seemingly tranquillising discourses and reciting extracts from religious texts.

The associates (close disciples), of the godmen leave no stone unturned in attracting more and more people at the pre-announced discourse venues. Most people (particularly the illiterate and women), make it a part of their life to attend such congregations and listen attentively to the discourses of these so-called godmen – the swamijis and babajis. The programmes and venues of these religious congregations are well advertised – even months in advance – in order to ensure huge gatherings. People, in hundreds of thousands, throng to such venues faithfully and listen to what the swamijis utter. They join their bhajan-singing parties, by perpetual clapping and loud singing.

Some of the so-called godmen or swamis, succeed at some time in becoming, high-profile entities, with a flood of followers at their backing. There have been a number of godmen who have boastfully claimed to have performed miracles with their spiritual powers and capabilities. People almost blindly take their claims as perfectly true. Streams of the followers of the godmen can be seen flowing in spate, at innumerable venues and times, the world over. Out of sheer ignorance, people can be seen to be attracted to the utterances of so many so-called godmen of high profile, because of their staunch belief in these godmen's spiritual capabilities. The close associates of these godmen float fabricated stories and incidents, highlighting the miracles performed by their godmen from time to time and unfortunately, most of the people take them as true and that makes them throng to the venues of the discourses.

Behind the overwhelming success of most of the godmen, one will find some politicians, or men in high places, with vested interests. These unsocial elements do not hesitate to invest huge sums of money in bringing their godmen into the limelight.

They organise gigantic congregations and get-togethers, with the help of their henchmen, who usually are bad characters - the so-called social workers, the area political party office-bearers, such as presidents and secretaries etc. Once they succeed in securing huge followings for their godmen, they get acres of land allotted to them at prime locations, at throwaway prices. They act in league with the men in authority for constructing ashrams and residential dwellings and even shops and business outlets (within the ashram campus). Then the people at the helm transplant their henchmen (the political rogues), in the garb of small godmen or 'swamis' in the ashram precincts. The wolves in lambs' clothing are given a free hand by their masters to indulge in all sorts of activities, with the sole aim of building assets for their masters, their godmen, as well as for themselves, by befooling the people at large, i.e. the blind followers. These mafia men apply all sorts of tricks and adopt unfair and ugly means, to raise more and more funds and acquire moveable and immovable assets for themselves and their mafia masters and godmen, as well as their close disciples, now saffron-clad, with a huge but fascinating 'tilak' on their foreheads and of course rosaries and rudraksh maalas around their necks. The followers of the swamijis frequently throng the ashrams for their *darshanas*—touching their feet and offering hefty *dakshinas* and above all, for getting their physical and mental problems solved.

The offerings in cash or kind are carefully collected by the *chelas* (disciples), of the godmen and are systematically shared by the mafia men. The major share goes to the kingpins (the politicians and their close associates).

The concluding decade of the twentieth century has witnessed a ruthless mushrooming of temples and ashrams on encroached government lands and public parks, at innumerable places – particularly in India, thanks to the political and public figures, being backed by the official bigwigs and of course, the law enforcers. Unfortunately, the people behind the land encroachments (mostly at prime locations), who are instrumental in getting the same allotted for a temple building or ashrams for high-profile godmen, are held in high esteem. These hypocrites call themselves social workers and claim to be doing something good for the oppressed and downtrodden, by converting public lands into temples and ashram complexes and also opening charitable trusts and dispensaries and other public conveniences. The people at large (the followers of the godmen), throng in hundreds and thousands daily, to seek blessings of the godmen and to get their physical and mental ills remedied, at these so-called ashrams and temples. These blind followers are either too illiterate or too simple, to get at the real motive of the persons behind the birth of such ashrams and temples, here and there. Really, there is no dearth of blind followers, particularly in India.

Then, there is also no dearth of fake swamijis, fortune-tellers, palmists and sadhus in saffron robes, in our present-day world. In order to find solutions to their problems and miseries, people from all walks of life, faithfully pay frequent visits to them—the so-called problem-solvers. They do not mind parting with hefty dakshinas (offerings), to the deputies of these gods, simply in order to search for solutions (*upais*) to their physical and mental problems.

These self-styled swamijis, in their saffron and yellow robes, rob them by suggesting hypothetical solutions (*upais*) to all sorts of worldly ills. The remedies suggested by these godly men (wolves in lambs' clothing), often prove costly and time-consuming. The irony is that most men and women, being illiterate and blind followers, undergo the process of '*upais*' strictly, as suggested by their problem-solvers. When they find their problems remaining unsolved for quite some time even after going through the process of upais, they start frequenting them (the swamijis etc.), in order to know the reasons for their problems remaining unsolved. These cunning godmen make them believe that the *upais* (remedies), suggested by them in the first instance had not been done as per *vidhies* (procedure). They then suggest that they do a fresh set of *upais* for which they are convinced to part, with hefty dakshinas again. In most cases, the cycle of upais and dakshinas goes on for quite a long time. And when they (the people with blind faith), find themselves back to square one every time, even after undergoing the process strictly, as per vidhi (procedure), they do not blame their problem-solvers (the godmen). They prefer to find fault in themselves assuming that the *upais* had not been done in the correct spirit.

However, in some cases some of the problems of the solution-seekers automatically get solved, with the passage of time. (In fact, the problems, as per nature's law, fade away one by one, in due course). But the credit goes to the swamijis – the so-called godmen, the problem-solvers. The persons whose problems get solved (of course, with the passage of time), tell their acquaintances and fellow beings that their problems have been overcome by the 'blessings' of their swamijis. Others, whose problems have remained unsolved (or partly solved), even after repeatedly seeking remedial measures from their swamiji, do not blame any godman. They find fault with their fate and not with their problem-solver. They simply prefer to curse their fate (instead of cursing their swamiji). Anyhow, the godmen and their like continue with their bluffing tactics and mint money at the cost of their innocent, blind followers and devotees. They continue to enjoy the patronage of their followers unabatedly.

These hypocrites leave no stone unturned in

maintaining their high-profile public image, in league with the political and power-hungry bigwigs. The fact is that these dangerous, unsocial, diabolic people (in the garb of godmen and social workers), indulge in all sorts of unsocial activities—from land-grabbing to building so-called ashrams, blackmailing, smuggling, extortions (in indirect ways), to even womanising etc.—all at the cost of most of their blind followers and corrupt business persons. All the scandals and scams plaguing the nation, take birth from them.

These hypocrites—the traitors (the poor, embodied souls), appear to be ignorant of the existence of the omnipotent, all-pervading natural forces, which meticulously react to the bad and good karmas of all living beings. But these unsocial elements go on with their deceitful, diabolic acts, undeterred and also probably not believing in the punishment (at the hands of the all-pervading natural forces), in lieu of their deceitful and bad karmas. Then a day comes when the omnipotent divine forces react to the deceitful acts of these soulless demons and make their universal existence felt. These subtle and gracious forces ultimately corner the evil ones, one by one, very very gradually, but surely.

I have never come across a diabolic person, (in the garb of a godman, a social politician, a hypocrite, or a man of authority), who flourished perennially, by embracing all sorts of deceitful acts, or who did not receive punishment at the hands of the all-pervading forces, for his crime (deceitful acts), against His creatures.

No embodied soul can escape from the clutches of the all-powerful celestial forces for its deceitful acts and misadventures.

The irony is that even the literate and men of high positions, such as MLAs, MPs, state governors, ministerial secretaries, government bigwigs and even chief ministers and prime ministers (to some extent), besides political leaders and high-profile businessmen, like to become disciples of some of the godmen who enjoy the patronage and respect of hundreds of thousands of followers from all all walks of life. These very important and famous people can be seen visiting various godmen and fortune-tellers—probably to know their instant fate, to know what is in store for them, in the times to come. Businessmen throng to them to know whether or not they would be gainers in a particular business deal. And men of high position, like MLAs, MPs, ministers, chief ministers, state governors, ministerial secretaries etc. patronise them and try to remain very close to them on various pretexts—from seeking blessings, to extracting huge benefits and monetary gains, by unfair means (in league with some of the high-profile godmen).

Ridiculously, these VIPs and famous men, believe in getting their fate interpreted by godmen or fortune-tellers. I am sure most of them do not believe in the basic principle of life which says, 'as you sow, so shall you reap'. What I mean to say is that they (the poor souls), do not understand that it is only their actions (good or bad), which are going to count.

Every embodied soul is accountable for his actions – the karmas. His destiny (or fate), perpetually goes on taking shape (changing), depending upon the good or bad karmas. Apparently, no fortune-teller or astrologer, or godman, can change one's fate or destiny to suit one's convenience or gain.

Man himself is the maker or destroyer of his fate

I wonder why even the well-educated and those holding key positions cannot understand the simple, natural phenomenon, of crime and punishment. Why do they run after fortune-tellers and godmen, for the rectification of their fate? Can't they understand that the divine, gracious natural forces, flawlessly (and meticulously), maintain the equilibrium of crime and punishment? Don't they know that there is punishment in store for them, in commensuration with the crime (evil karmas), they commit? To my mind, such people are either sceptical of the great natural phenomenon of crime and punishment, or are completely deluded by materialism. They appear to take refuge in the physical gains and comforts of high places only. They are certainly the lost, embodied souls, who cannot go in for introspection.

People at large staunchly believe in taking a dip in the holy Ganges, particularly at Har Ki Pauri in Haridwar, Varanasi ghats, Brahma sarovers (in Kurukshetra), and in so many other sarovers and sacred waters, located at innumerable places, so as to get themselves purged of all their sins. They probably feel highly satisfied after taking their dips in holy waters (particularly in the Ganga), as they become sure they have been purged of their sins and misadventures. What a blind faith! This, in other words, means that one first goes on committing sins the way one likes and then gets purified and purged of one's sins and crimes at any time—in one go—by simply taking a so-called holy dip.

Those who believe in this hypothetical way of getting rid of their sins are perhaps, the most disillusioned souls on earth. That means they are licensed to commit sins and crime as they (as per their belief), ultimately are surely going to get purged of all their sins in one go, by just taking a holy dip. Perhaps this is one of the factors contributing to the everyday increase in all sorts of sins, including heinous crime. Such blind faith is resulting in the birth of more and more criminals, as we all must sincerely acknowledge. The hard fact remains that taking dips in holy waters, wearing rings of various metals and precious stones (on the fortune-teller's advice), wearing *taweez* or rudraksh maalas, undertaking pilgrimages to holy places, chanting of mantras (without knowing their meanings), visiting holy shrines frequently, bowing before man-made gods and so-called godmen, again and again touching the feet of swamis, yellow-robed sadhus, temple priests etc.—is in no way going to help one in getting rid of one's problems, miseries and above all—one's sins. God does not accept the prayers of those who do not desist from committing bad karmas and all sorts of sins. What really counts is one's actions only. All shall be well if one's actions are good, in the truest sense. How can the holy dips and wearing of metals and stones and rudraksh maalas, purge one of one's sins and make one rich and problem-free if one's actions are bad and harmful to one's fellow beings? We are not going to be pardoned by the forces around us for one's perennial sinful karmas and deceitful acts. And if one is really virtuous and harmless creature, one is surely, sooner or later, going to be rewarded (compensated), for one's miseries by the divine forces, in unique ways. If one is not a good man, one should not expect any good in return. This is the supreme celestial law. There is no escape. The universally acknowledged maxims (proverbs)—'do good and have good'; 'as one sow, so shall one reap'—are certainly not vague or meaningless. These have been divinely proved ever true. One cannot be at peace if one has failed to keep His creatures at peace. How can one remain problem free if one has remained a problem maker?

Chapter VIII

Man's journey from his birth to his natural death, as we all know, is extremely gradual and slow. This is so, because nature's process is always slow and time-consuming but, undoubtedly, most systematic and flawless. 'The sun is stationary'—this is a universal truth and is scientifically proved, too. But still, we human beings treat it, or call it, a moving celestial object by saying, 'the sun has risen', 'the sun has set'. And yet again, we often say that the sun rises in the east and sets in the west after completing its day's journey. We can thus authentically say the sun's journey from 'day-dawn' to 'day-dusk' is very very gradual, slow but sure. If the day has dawned, the day-dusk is certain.

It is, of course, our earth that rotates on its axis and completes one rotation in every twenty-four hours. It is apparently the earth's rotation that causes days and nights. Again, it is the earth that moves round the sun in its orbit, at an amazing speed of nineteen kilometres per second, completing the journey (each cycle), in one year, five hours and forty-nine minutes—thus giving birth to various seasons, i.e. summer, winter, spring and autumn. But surely, this movement of the celestial bodies is perennial, flawless and amazingly accurate. And again, the moon, being the earth's satellite, moves around the earth with utmost accuracy.

To sum up, we human beings authentically believe, without the slightest doubt, that the stars, the moon, the earth and innumerable planets – all celestial bodies, millions of miles away from one another – perennially move, rise or set, in an immaculate, automatic and flawless celestial system, giving birth to days, nights, seasons and weathers. The entire universal order thus makes us believe how amazing and stunning our *brahmand* is. And what is more amazing is that all the heavenly bodies perpetually exist in perfect co-ordination under the supreme, celestial order.

The movement of these heavenly bodies however is amazingly swift, flawlessly punctual, but appears to us extremely slow. We cannot see these bodies moving with our naked eyes. That is why they appear to our eyes as stationary. The irony is how many of us have the time to ponder over the amazing secrets of the celestial bodies? How disciplined the heavenly bodies are! Do we ever seriously think of this most wonderful natural phenomenon?

Coming back to the nature's slow process – take the example of seasons – summer does not come overnight and neither do the other seasons such as winter, spring or autumn. The change in seasons or weather, is very very gradual and time consuming. We can see summer gradually fading away to autumn, autumn to winter, winter to spring and spring to summer.

Can a child be born in a day? Can all the mammals deliver their babies overnight? Can we reap the crop sown, a day earlier? Or, can we consume our whole life's food in a day? It takes, as we all know, nine months for a human baby to born. Mammals, too, deliver their babies in a specified time, that varies from mammal to mammal. Similarly, the process from the sowing of seeds to the harvesting of crops is carried out step by step; it is time-consuming—spanning several months. Fruits do not ripen in a day and become eatable. Hair do not grow in a day. The embodied souls (all living beings), do not get old in a day. Man's journey of life, from his birth to his death, as we all know, passes through various inevitable stages—each time-consuming. He has to cross all the stages; right from his birth to infancy, infancy to childhood, childhood to adolescence, adolescence to youth, youth to dotage and finally dotage to his death. All these take their own time. All these stages span years and decades. All living beings, whether in human body or in any other form of life, have to pass through all these stages of life—ultimately leading to a common destination—inevitable death. Nature, gradually but surely, goes on consuming the embodied soul, by making it pass through various stages, before finally pushing it to the jaws of death.

All this clearly suggests that the divine, universal order is flawless, immaculate, non-stop, extremely gradual, but inevitable in its entirety.

This phenomenon of nature thus teaches us the lesson of patience. Unfortunately, the people at large lack it in one way or the other.

Lack of patience, in fact, is a nature-born phenomenon. It is the baby of materialism which gives rise to anger and ego. And these two elements emanate from a lack of real knowledge (the wisdom), which is the cardinal cause of all one's physical and mental ills. Anger thus, is man's greatest enemy. It ultimately carries him to the threshold of hell, via incurable physical and mental diseases, loss of reasoning and finally loss of memory. Thus man is himself the real source of his sufferings.

If one sincerely acknowledges it, one must admit that one cannot get certain things done at the press of a button. And when things are not done according to one's wishes, one at times, get furious, which is the other name of 'anger' (as well as ego). Divine forces will not permit one to do certain things of one's own volition. They won't let one go astray the way one likes. It is not necessary that one's 'will' will always prevail. The forces will certainly not let one overstep barriers, undeterred and unharmed. They will react at the most appropriate moments to one's malicious advances.

Chapter IX

One of my close acquaintances was an alcoholic. I saw him consuming about a bottle of liquor almost daily, after sunset. He used to have drinking sessions in the company of his brothers-in-law, as well as some other close acquaintances, at the cost of the comfort of his family members. The drinking sessions used to last till the late evening hours. His drinking habit spanned nearly three decades. Then he was also in the habit of playing cards with his fellow drunkards up to late in the night and that too, almost daily. He appeared to have no respect for the night, which, in fact, as per nature's law, is meant for taking rest and sleeping, after the day's hard work. He had no regard for his family members either. What I minutely observed was that his spouse and all his five children were awfully afraid of his habit of shouting, at the slightest pretext. He used to get wild and out of control, shouting and created ugly scenes. Hot words were exchanged daily, between him and his spouse. At times, cards and drinking sessions used to last the whole night. They used to light candles when the electricity failed, during their card-playing sessions.

I repeatedly requested him to check his drinking and card-playing habits and tried to persuade him to come down to decent limits. I don't think my requests had any effect on him. He appeared not to be in need of anybody's advice. He thus continued undeterred and unbridled, with these two habits, for many many years. And then, a stage came when the results of his ruthless consumption of alcohol and non-stop card-playing, started surfacing. The natural forces now had started reacting to his trespassing and inhumane behaviour. He gradually developed a chronic pain in his abdomen. Medical treatment had little effect. He started growing physically weak, day by day. Further deterioration in his health now prevented him from playing cards, till the late night hours. Gradually, he became physically too weak to spend many hours on his perennial drinking and cards habits. But the *lakshman rekha* appeared to have been crossed. The forces were now reciprocating his misadventures. A stage came, when he could be seen suffering terribly from insomnia. In his mid-fifties, I saw him often consuming about five or six sleeping tablets, just to ensure a couple of hours' sleep. He had, at this stage, stopped playing cards but his drinking habit continued unabated. He was at one time seen spending money like water, towards his medical treatment.

I saw his health completely shattered when he was on the wrong side of the fifties. And I also saw him staggering, while walking or talking. However, his ego, even at this belated stage, did not diminish. This state of affairs continued for a few more years. He had become physically too weak to handle the liabilities of his business, which at one time used to be quite a roaring one. I had now stopped meeting him, for more than one reason. I, as well as my kin, were no longer on speaking terms with him or his kin, because of his indecent behaviour and rude temperament. To maintain his lavish lifestyle, he now started working on malicious designs to extract money from his in-laws, on one pretext or the other. He had, so to say, turned into a beast, because of his ill-intentioned and ill-motivated designs. All his children had left him one by one, as they grew up and got married. His spouse developed an incurable disease and ultimately died, after a few years' struggle with life. Despite all this, his ego remained with him, like his best friend.

Time rolled by. I was, however, kept informed about his dwindling ego day by day, by one of my close acquaintances who was quite close to him also. A few more years rolled by. Sleeping pills had now stopped helping him. The forces had been making their presence – or rather their existence – felt, by gradually cornering him. He was confronting the reactions to his actions (which are proven to be equal and opposite). He had been disrespectful to the nights. Now, the nights were disrespectful to him, by snatching his sleep. The divine forces, in their flawless natural phenomenon, were retaliating against his malicious advances and egoism.

One day I came to know from one of my close sources that his health had deteriorated to the point of no return and that he was now leading, by and large, a hellish life—all alone, in his one-time vibrant, luxury apartment. My informant also told me that his apartment now wore a deserted look—devoid of any hustle and bustle. He further told me that he often saw him madly drunk and crying in physical and mental pain, cursing God and his fate, unremorsefully. There was, he further added, no one present to console him, or to wipe his tears, or to share his drinks. A dreadful silence, he continued, was prevalent—no shouts, no laughters, no fellow-drunkards, no card-playing. Bottles of wine appeared to be his only companion, like a best friend. His luxury house now looked like a haunted house.

Cornered by the invisible, all-pervading, gracious but mysterious forces, he was surely reaping what he had sown.

The forces spare no one. They won't let one go scot-free and unpunished. For one's negative-traited actions and malicious designs, one will have to 'reap' one day what one has sown, sooner or later.

Chapter X

Human beings generally curse themselves and their fate, while in trouble. But at the same time, they blindly attribute their miseries simply to God's will. Instead of getting at the cause of their ills, they prefer to take these as preordained and inevitable. The poor souls do not know that their impure acts, emanating out of sheer negative traits, are the cause of their sufferings. Man, in fact, is himself the major source of his sufferings.

Divine forces keep on punishing us, in innumerable mysterious ways, from time to time, for our indulgence in bad karmas that take birth from our negative traits. Man, after all, is a blend of virtues and vices. The forces thus meticulously keep on rewarding and punishing him, at the appropriate moments. It is thus apparent that our joys and sorrows, at varying moments and spells, are inevitable.

One can avert mishaps (physical and mental problems), to a considerable extent, by shunning vices and embracing virtues. One's destiny thus keeps on changing perennially, depending upon one's karmas (actions). If one's actions are pure, one will have a cheerful, problem-free phase, at the right time. Similarly, one will have to face problematic and miserable phases for one's negative-traited actions. Thus we can draw the inference that leading a hellish life, or a blissful life, is to a considerable extent, in one's own hands. It thus depends upon oneself, whether one wants to remain problem-free or problem-infested, for most of one's lifetime.

As a natural rule, there are more sorrows than joys, more obstacles than smooth sailing, for all living beings, irrespective of whether they are in human body or in a beast's body. But one can certainly avert a number of one's mishaps and bad times and ensure having more blissful spells than sorrowful ones, by keeping oneself on the positive-traited track.

One is surely, the architect of one's destiny. This destiny is not immutable. It is ever-changing, depending upon one's performance. One can change one's circumstances by adhering to one's positive traits. One should not curse one's fate. There is a proverb - 'Whosoever curses his fate, his fate also keeps on cursing him.' So, be a hero in the strife and fight back the onslaughts of your vices valiantly. Don't be taken in by the fortune-tellers, pandits, peers, self-styled godmen, the so-called problem-solvers etc. In a bid to find solutions and remedies for one's problems and miseries, one is the greatest healer of one's worldly ills and problems, by shunning one's negative traits and embracing the positive ones.

Chapter XI

The mysterious forces keep on sending meaningful signals to the embodied souls every now and then. It depends entirely upon the individual, as to whether he is celestially equipped to receive such significant divine signals.

There are beings, very rare of course, who are divinely blessed, who catch these signals and interpret the same, with amazing accuracy. And, there are those who can partially catch these signals, devoid of their significance.

However, the people at large—the poor souls—are sceptical of these heavenly, transmitted signals. They do not believe in the existence of any such signal in their physical world.

And there are those, rarest of the rare, of course, who are in constant touch with these signals. It seems as though they are carrying out their worldly liabilities; (mandatory physical activities), constantly, at the behest of these heavenly signals. To such amiable souls, each and every signal conveys some meaningful message. Such people are celestially bestowed with the power of knowing, in the truest sense, the meaning of these signals and on the basis of such signals, they can accurately predict the ensuing events and also become instruments at times, for averting certain mishaps, or natural calamities.

Chapter XII

In the early eighties of the twentieth century, I found myself awfully busy in constructing a residential dwelling for my close kin. During those days, I was passing through, perhaps, one of the most critical phases of my life. I was in need of substantial funds to complete the construction of the house. As such, I had to raise the funds from more than one source, besides my entire savings. Whatever money I managed to raise from various sources, was exhausted almost completely by the time the construction was nearing completion. I was informed by one of my in-laws that as per an understanding, I would be getting ten thousand rupees from one of my relatives, in order to complete the house. However, they did not tell me the time (or date), and place, of his delivering the money to me.

It was a pleasant, bright, sunny, winter day. I was sitting on a cot at the construction site, worrying about the progress of the work that had slowed down, because of paucity of funds. All of a sudden, I had an illusion. I felt as though I was catching an inexplicable, unique signal—telling me about the arrival shortly, of a relative of mine, along with his spouse, to deliver the money I was in need of. I got anxious to see whether there was really any truth in what I had envisioned moments earlier. And, wonderfully, it came true, within half-an-hour. My relative, accompanied by his spouse, landed at my construction site. After exchanging pleasantries, he told me he had come to deliver the money I badly needed, for completing the remaining work. He took out ten thousand rupees from his pocket and handed it over to me. I was inwardly thankful to him as well as to the all-pervading, helping forces. I have ever remained grateful to them both.

On a summer morning, I was, as per my daily routine, busy getting ready to leave for my place of work. After getting rid of all the mandatory exercises (activities), I finally extended my hand on the top of our refrigerator for my specs. It did not come in my hand. Soon, I realised it was not lying there. Never had it happened so, as I consider myself an extremely careful and alert person, as regards all my activities of everyday life. I always ensure the safe custody of my every day use articles, such as identity cards, bunch of keys, pens, watch, hankie, goggles and the spectacles. Anyhow, I kept on searching my specs for some time. But, as I was getting late, I took the old one (the obsolete, not much helpful) and left for my duty. I felt a lot of discomfort in discharging my official liabilities, involving writing and reading, the whole day, because of its obsolete lenses. On my return from the office (in the late evening hours, as usual), I made another desperate attempt to trace the missing specs. I searched all the nooks and corners of the house; but my specs were nowhere in sight. It made me uncomfortable as I could neither watch TV, nor read the newspaper. I made yet another attempt the following morning but it all proved futile. It made me irritated somewhat. Again (on the second day), I had to be content with my old specs and once again, I devoted quite some time after I was back from my office, but I miserably failed in my attempts to trace it. I had now decided to go in for fresh eye-sight testing and spectacles, the very next morning. I retired to my bed without watching TV or reading the newspaper, as I had done on the preceding day.

In the early morning of the following day, I had a strange but significant dream—a dream I never had had before. In the dream, I saw my specs resting distinctly on a rusty, metallic surface, covered with dust. As I got up in the morning, I had no difficulty in recollecting what I had dreamt a few hours earlier. What perturbed me was that I had not seen any such rusty, metallic surface, in my household. Even so, I started searching for the specs afresh. About half-an-hour's search proved futile, I felt as if I were wasting my time. Then, all of a sudden, something which cannot be explained in words made me go upstairs to the *mumty* (landing at the top of a flight of stairs). I then went to the terrace and surveyed it minutely. There was nothing resembling a rusted, metallic surface. As I was getting late, I hastily came to the mumty door. The moment I entered the mumty, I saw some old, discarded household articles lying in a spacious corner, by the side of the mumty door. In the moments that ensued, my eyes fell on an old, rusted trunk, which I could not recollect if I had ever seen and I was wonderstruck to see my specs lying on its dusty surface— in the very position in which I had seen them, in my wee-hour dream. Stunned, I picked them up and thanked Him. I had never thought a dream could also come true. I attributed this incident to the divine signal that had been transmitted to me, in my sleep, in the shape of a dream. It did not take me much time to recollect that I had been to the terrace a couple of days back, to ensure that the mumty door was properly locked. Never before had I imagined that a dream could also come true. This incident kept me wonderstruck for quite some time. In all my life till then, that was the only dream that had come true, in such an amazing way.

Chapter XIII

I was stationed along with a few colleagues at a place in one of the remotest areas of Nepal, for a little over four years, in the late seventies and early eighties. We used to be virtually cut off from the rest of the world during the monsoon season, which lasted five months every year. In the year 1980, I received a telegram from my home town in India, informing me of my father's demise. I was not surprised that I had received the telegram after fourteen days of my father's death as the area I was stationed at, was really very remote and hard to access.

Anyhow, with the greatest difficulty, I managed to reach my home town. All the post-death rites were over by the time I arrived there. Thus, after spending a few days with my mother, brothers, sisters etc. I set out for my return journey. If took me nine days to get back to my remote station. All went well for three days after my return. On the fourth day, I had the most amazing and horrible experience, in the wee hours of a dark, starry night. I was sleeping (as usual), in my bedroom in my semi-pucca camp dwelling, which was surrounded by forests and hillocks. I was awakened by a mournful murmur and the cries of someone. I at once got up from my bed, walked up to my window and gazed outside, to make sure that I was really awake and not dreaming. The peculiar murmur and crying, though not so loud, was certainly frightening. I tried to locate the direction from which the peculiar, inexplicable mournful cries were coming. My judgement took me to the rear verandah. I stepped onto the verandah, and was terribly frightened when I came across what looked like the shadow of a man, a few yards away, crying and murmuring as if he was in great mental agony. I tried to catch the utterances of the shadowy figure. With the passing of a few moments, I was able to catch the murmur. In great mental agony it kept repeating, 'O lord, why it is so? Why such great mental punishment? What should I do? What should I do?' It did not take me much time to realise that the shadowy figure was none other than my dead father. It exactly resembled him. I was too frightened to immediately react. The figure gradually faded into nothingness. As I came back to my bed, the shadow started appearing again and with the same murmuring cries. However, after a few moments, it vanished. I collected some courage and lit the hurricane lantern which was lying in a corner of the verandah. The light confirmed that I was really awake, as I did not get any sleep in the remaining early morning hours, after that dreadful, harrowing experience, which had lasted about ten or twelve minutes. However, one thing is certain. This peculiar and terrifying happening further brought me close to the secrets of divine nature—the all-pervading, mysterious forces, encasing us.

Chapter XIV

Some of my contemporaries—my colleagues of the sixties and seventies—flourished immensely, right before my eyes, in a short span of time—not by dint of hard work alone but by embracing all sorts of unfair means and malpractices. Their sole aim appeared to be to amass more and more wealth, by hook or by crook.

I was often severely criticised by my kith and kin for not making hay while the sun shone. They called me a 'backward' as I could not spin money, by embracing corruption and malpractices. At times I used to be labelled a pauper, who failed to keep pace with the changing times. They often used to quote the examples of some of my contemporaries who had been heading towards the accumulation of riches at breakneck speed. Within a couple of years of their entering into service, some of my colleagues had their own comfortable dwellings, besides their own motor-driven vehicles. They had managed quite a good number of amenities, for a comfortable living. To sum up, they appeared to be flourishing and flourishing by leaps and bounds.

I had lagged behind because of my sincerity in carrying out my assigned obligations. And secondly, my inner self did not permit me to indulge in any unfair means. I was, thus, leading the life of an average man, by the then living standards. But I had enough mental peace and satisfaction as compared to those colleagues of mine who had become rich (by hook or by crook). I often used to tell my spouse and children that we would also be having our own comfortable house as well as the amenities and privileges of a modern life, some day. They did not appear to have any faith in these utterances of mine.

The most critical phase of my life, which lasted about fifteen years, saw my children receiving good quality education, in reputed public schools and me raising loans from various sources to construct a home and also repay loans in monthly instalments, spanning several years. During these fifteen years, we were virtually living from hand to mouth. I was very particular about getting my children educated in reputed public schools, despite my financial constraints.

Anyway, the years rolled by, one by one, and a day came when I saw my eldest child securing a good job in a private concern of national repute, almost immediately after completing his graduation in commerce. With his employment, our financial position improved a little. Then my wife, who, too, is an educated lady, got a teaching job in the same public school in which my two daughters were still receiving their education. With her employment, which was on a yearly agreement basis, our financial position improved further. The ensuing months saw me promoted to a responsible position, resulting in a handsome increase in my emoluments. We no longer felt financially hard up. To sum up, I can truthfully say that in a span of about eight months, our financial status changed amazingly. No longer did we belong to the lower middle class. I attribute this sudden change in financial status to the blessings of the wonderful, gracious forces, which react commensurately to our positive and negative traits, at the most appropriate time. I staunchly believe that these subtle forces ultimately come to our rescue (after making us pass through our struggles and critical phases), in response to our positive actions—the pure karmas.

And a day also came when I saw all my three children settled lucratively, in companies of international repute, on highly responsible positions. The mid-nineties saw me as well as my family members leading a high-profile lifestyle with all the requisite amenities, by the grace of the all-powerful, celestial forces.

I also saw some of my contemporaries of the sixties and seventies, who had left me far behind then, in acquiring material and physical comforts, leading a desperate life, on various and varying counts. Some of them were seen to be suffering from mental agonies at the hands of their grown-up, unbridled children. Others were suffering intensely from chronic diseases. They apparently appeared dejected because of their failure to lead a healthy, problem-free and prosperous life, in the concluding period of their physical existence.

Thus, we can draw an inference from what we see in our life. The amiable, despite their crises and critical phases, spanning many years—even decades in some cases, ultimately come out victorious. At the same time, the evil and negative-traited ones, who, in the beginning, seemed to be flourishing (by unfair means), by leaps and bounds, in the active part of their life, come out the losers in the last run. And this is what the basic principle of life is—'As you sow, so shall you reap.'

The omniscient and all-pervading forces, encasing each and every embodied soul, strictly and meticulously enforce this perennial, basic law, in countless ways. There is no escape. Nobody on earth can be above this supreme law. Freedom of Will will not work beyond its limitations. Overstepping or setting aside the natural barriers would mean confronting the omnipotent forces. If one breaks the natural barriers, the forces will retaliate, by breaking one at the most appropriate time. Too much materialism allures violation of natural barriers. But these barriers won't let one go unharmed when one chooses to ignore them. Obviously, too much materialism is a curse. It's a curse in disguise.

Men of wisdom know this very well. They do understand, in the real sense, what is good for them and what is not good for them. These amiable souls staunchly believe in serving the tormented and wounded souls. They feel mentally satisfied in remaining compassionate to their fellow beings, rather than wasting much time in worldly materialism. They keep their ego at bay and continue undeterred, in mitigating the miseries of His creatures. They do not waste much time in visiting places of worship and pleasing gods in blind ways, unlike most of their fellow beings. Rather, they believe in serving the tormented, embodied souls, as His true servants.

Chapter XV

I visited Mussoorie for the first time, in December, 1965. After a couple of days' stay I had to beat a hasty retreat as the weather had suddenly become inclement. I can never forget the bitter experience I had, on my first day at the queen of hills. What happened and what went wrong with me, on that day, goes like this—

I was loitering all alone, on the beautiful, clean roads, of the hill town, enjoying nature's beauty. I happened to pass by the side of Gun-Hill, the highest peak of the town, from the top of which, a cannon used to be fired at a fixed hour in the evening, during the British era. However, the gun had stopped booming with the cessation of British rule.

The peak of Gun-Hill allured me to scale it. Instead of going atop by a metalled path meant for tourists, I preferred an alternative route, a shortcut, to reach the top. It was a narrow, unpaved path (pagdandi), that appeared to be zigzagging up to the top, somewhat steeply. As I reached mid-point, I was dismayed to find my chosen 'pagdandi' dwindling into non-existence. I came to a grinding halt somewhat nervously. I became motionless for a short spell. I then started exploring the possibility of climbing down to the starting point. As I turned back to see whether I could go down safely, I was completely taken aback when my eyes failed to see the path I had chosen to climb up by. Down below, I could see only the deep valley of Dehradun, partially covered with mist. This view made me perspire and feel nervous. My immediate judgement told me that I could neither climb up, nor go down, to my starting point, unharmed.

I closed my eyes for a few moments to overcome my nervousness and vertigo. I succeeded in overcoming these two things to some extent and decided to resume the upward climb, by sheer judgement. As I went up a few more yards, another obstacle, of a grave nature overtook me. I found myself stepping on a soil covered with loose, pebble-like ingredients. And as I went up a few more steps, a huge chunk of the loose soil mixed with tiny pebbles slid down, taking me along with it. Perhaps this was the moment when I prayed to God from the core of my heart, to spare my life. He, I am extremely sure, accepted my prayer. There was a huge rock about forty feet below which checked my descent and that of the loose soil. The soil kept being deposited by the broad shoulders of the rock. I also got deposited by it in the company of the huge chunk of sliding soil. I felt quite safe now. I relaxed for some time.

As I looked up to the top of the hill, I saw some people looking down at me. They seemed aware of what was happening. They waved their hands. It made me confident of getting some sort of help. And then my eyes fell on a metal pipe a few feet away from where I had been deposited. With some effort, I caught hold of this pipe, which helped me to scale the hill, up to a fairly decent height. The pipe vanished at one point. It went underground. And then I was amazed to see a narrow path (pagdandi), just in front of me. I followed it step-by-step with all due caution. In minutes I found myself at the top of the hill. The people at the top appeared to be anxiously waiting for my safe arrival. They told me that the moment they saw me trapped mid-way, they had sent a message down to the fire brigade.

A few minutes later the fire brigade, appearing fully equipped to cope with any eventuality, landed at the scene. They were satisfied to see that all was okay. I thanked them profusely for the promptness with which they had performed their duty. I thanked the people, too, who had lost no time in sending down the message to the fire-brigade people the moment they saw me trapped mid-way, on the steep slopes of Gun Hill.

I was inwardly immensely grateful to the omniscient and all-pervading gracious forces which (under His supreme command), saved my life. I felt as though I had been bestowed a fresh lease of life by Him.

I learnt a lesson from this incident. 'Always adhere to the right path in your life's journey.'

Off the track

A true saint won't let you touch his feet.

Chapter XVI

You must have come across many people embracing superstitions. For example, some men do not shave or get their hair cut on Tuesdays and Thursdays.

Many women do not wash their hair, or clothes, on Thursdays. Some do not consume onions or garlic on Tuesdays. And there are many who do not consume the morning cup of tea—the so-called 'bed-tea'—before taking a bath in holy water, on particular days. Many among devout Hindus are very particular about taking dips in sacred waters such as the Ganga, the Brahma Sarover, the Triveni etc., on the days of solar eclipses and the New Year day of the Hindu calendar.

Some materialists display symbols such as *shubh labham* on the front doors, or walls of their houses, shops and business places. Others display words like *Om* (or its symbol), *Jai Maa, Jai Bajrang,* God is Love, Lord Bless Me, *Ek Tera Sahara, Waheguru, Khuda Hafiz, Jai Maa Kali, Jai Mata Di,* Shiva, *Jai Hanuman, Jai Baba Gang Nath, Sai Baba, Sat Guru Teri Oat, Jai Bhawani, Jai Maa Durge,* Rama Krishna, *Hare Krishna* and so many other, similar words, on the front and rear windscreens of their motor cars and other mechanically driven vehicles. There is absolutely no harm in displaying such auspicious words and symbols, provided those who display such symbols are amiable and truly God-fearing. But what about those who, by their very nature, are impure in their thoughts and actions and are full of moral blemishes? For such people, any such displays on their cars are meaningless.

I fail to understand why they display these auspicious

words and symbols on their windscreens when they are inwardly very well aware that they are morally corrupt and harmful to their fellow beings, in countless ways. Do they think they remain physically protected by Him, by simply displaying auspicious words and symbols on their vehicles? Or, do they feel they would remain ever safe with such displays and would continue to go scot-free, after committing sins each time?

Taking dips in holy waters, no doubt, is considered auspicious and soul-purifying, as per a popular belief among the Hindus. But, taking such holy baths shall only be meaningful if the bather resolves to become virtuous and pure in his actions (karmas), after taking the holy dip and thereafter, remains ever remorseful for the sins he had been committing from time to time. This is the best and surest way of getting purified. There is no point in taking holy dips, particularly on auspicious days, if one is not prepared to shun one's bad acts and embrace virtues.

The irony is that people at large pay little heed to this natural phenomenon. Their holy dips thus become devoid of any meaning. Only the rare, pure souls, know truly the purpose of taking holy dips. These noble, embodied souls, pledge to remain perpetually pure – in their thoughts and karmas - at the time of their holy dips. Thus, taking holy dips blindly, every now and then, without shunning sinful acts is of no use. It amounts to a sheer blind act, devoid of any significance.

Many men and women observe fasts on different days and auspicious occasions. Some observe them on Mondays, some on Tuesdays and some others on Saturdays.

I have come across some people who, otherwise non-vegetarians, become vegetarians on the days of their fast. Some staunch non-vegetarians become pure vegetarians only on auspicious days. And there are people who do not believe in shunning non vegetarian food on any day of the year. There are people (of course, small in number), who, perhaps do not believe in becoming temporarily vegetarian on any auspicious day of the year. They stick to their non-vegetarian diets under all circumstances. And yet they claim to be staunch Hindus, like anybody else.

I have often come across a number of my acquaintances, both close and distant, and my relatives, and their spouses, who observe auspicious days and occasions quite enthusiastically (even strictly as per religious codes), and some even become temporary *tilakdharies* and teetotallers, but without dissociating themselves from their blemishes. They continue to remain hypocritical and conceited and a menace to their fellow beings, in a number of ways. To my mind, such people are simply hypocrites and have come into this world only to nourish themselves. They are not expected to be compassionate to their fellow beings. No good can be expected to be delivered by these poor souls. I have often observed many people of this type frequenting places of worship, participating in religious congregations, chanting mantras loudly, wearing spotless white, or saffron kurta-pyjamas, with rosaries around their necks, and conspicuously present on auspicious occasions. They can be seen indulging in dirty politics with their political colleagues—the presidents, vice presidents, secretaries, treasurers and executives of the temple management—after the rituals are over. Instead of inculcating virtues in them, they involve themselves deeply in sectarianism and mudslinging on their antagonists (political rivals). A sort of tug of war for an esteemed office among various groups, is a common sight in the present-day management of the places of worship.

The hard fact is that egoists and hypocrites are controlling the affairs of temples (the places of worship). What goodness can they be expected to deliver to society?

Misappropriation of temple funds by the members of the managing committees has become very common. Religious places have, by and large, become the battlefields of politics. The managers of religious places have become power drunk. The really good members of the managing committees have become insignificant in management affairs. They have no say in the corrupt atmosphere of today. The malignant members of the management committee of a temple, or a place of worship, are generally to be seen in the majority. They keep themselves silently engaged in putting their amiable management colleagues in embarrassing positions, on one pretext or the other by adopting all sorts of ugly tricks. The amiable members, being small in number, in today's scene can be seen facing a series of setbacks at the hands of their deceitful, shrewd, management colleagues. Thus, a tug of war goes on perennially, between the two or more distinct groups, managing the affairs of the places of worship. In this war, the malicious members, in the garb of God's deputies, triumph over the amiable ones, most of the time.

Group politics in management can often be observed by anyone on the lines of caste and financial status. There are the Brahmins, the Rajputs, the Baniyas, the Kashtriyas etc. as well as the rich, the upper middle class, the middle class and the poor. The amiable members, in general, come from the middle class and poor category. These noble ones, irrespective of their caste, creed and financial status, can be seen sticking to their nature-borne, positive traits, despite their minority and humiliating onslaughts of their hypocritical management colleagues. They, no doubt, remain on a losing spree in their war against their conceited colleagues, during most of their membership tenure, but do not deviate from the lofty heights of idealism. Under no circumstances do they feel compelled to embrace hypocrisy, or to surrender to their shrewd colleagues.

However, it would not be out of place to mention that there are always exceptions everywhere, in every sphere, as per one of the fundamental principles of nature. It is, therefore, certainly not true that all the rich, or high-caste, are hypocritical and deceitful. Nor is it true that all the poor or middle class, or the non-Brahmins, are amiable. The exceptions are always there. But in general, the rich and affluent can be seen embracing vanity and hypocrisy while the poor and the middles embracing virtues and humility by and large as far as the management of the places of worship are concerned. Despite all these odds, the funds for running the temples, places of worship, *dharamshalas, ashrams,* etc. come from the pockets of these rich and affluent. Perhaps that is why this affluent group continues to exist. After all, they are doing something, be it in the shape of money, for the temples and for society. The forces treat them somewhat leniently.

I am sorry, my dear readers, that I have strayed somewhat from my point. I simply wanted to say that most of the places of worship, irrespective of caste, creed or religion, have mushroomed and are ruthlessly mushrooming out of the funds flowing from the pockets of the rich and the affluent—albeit for their own vested interests. An average worshipper has nothing to do with the controversial issues of who is funding or who is looking after the religious places. They appear to be too simple to bother about these things. They seem to be concerned with the worshipping of their gods and goddesses, who they believe, live in the temples only.

Doesn't one feel that the foundations of most of our religious places are laid on black money and vested interests?

Off The Track

A house in which the prayer hour of the lady of the house clashes with the breakfast hour, is a house that is devoid of peace and bliss.

Chapter XVII

I shall now be telling you about a man who had been consuming liquor heavily, besides smoking about sixty sticks of cigarettes and about a score of betel leaves (blended with a heavy dose of tobacco), each day, for nearly three decades and how he became a teetotaller overnight, with a vow not to touch liquor again, for the rest of his life.

Kanwar was a petty contractor by profession. He had been keeping company with drunkards right from his early twenties. He came in touch with me in his early forties and got very close to me, because of his profession. At one time I became fully aware of his becoming an addict. His drunkard colleagues, too, had crossed all decent limits and had become addicts like him. He, no doubt, had earned a lot from contracts but his awful drinking habit gradually swallowed his entire savings and earnings. A stage came when he had become bankrupt, pushing his dependants into severe financial constraints. The ensuing years saw him raising loans against the gold ornaments of his spouse, on tough terms, simply to overcome the prevalent financial crisis. During all those years, I had been warning this man, from time to time, about his approaching bleak days, if he did not stop drinking. My advice did not work as he had reached the point of no return. I had developed a lot of sympathy for him (because of some really good qualities and positive traits in him), but I had failed to help him get rid of his addiction. My repeated advice and warnings did not make any impact. His family members were completely shaken, over their only bread winner's reluctance to give up drinking, even under the worst financial crisis. And a time came when I saw him head over ears in debt. People around him had stopped lending him money.

He had now started coming home after midnight, almost daily, dead drunk, creating a nuisance and sometimes very ugly scenes.

As I saw him crossing all limits, I became dead sure that the natural celestial forces would now strike and check his non-stop, undeterred advances. Sure enough, that came out true. The gracious forces had now come to his, as well as his family member's rescue.

Kanwar was to attend a marriage at an outstation venue—about forty kilometres from his house.

After attending to his routine business, he came to a common place—an office (as usual), at noon, where his fellow-addicts had been waiting for him impatiently. Soon the afternoon drinking session started. They kept on drinking till evening. Immediately after sunset, he, along with his two fellow drunkards, who were very close to him, left for the venue of the marriage ceremony, in a van of one of his drunkard colleagues. The trio did not stop drinking during the journey either. They joined the marriage party awfully drunk. They were staggering, while exchanging pleasantries. At the marriage ceremony venue too, they continued consuming liquor, in the company of a few other invitees.

Kanwar, as per a rough estimate, had consumed about two bottles of liquor by the time of his departure from that place. As he was about to leave, he got an unbearable, sudden attack of pain in his stomach, that made him most uneasy. He requested his drinking partners to take him to a doctor, or a nursing home, for emergency medical aid, which he was badly in need of. The duo refused to oblige him, on the plea that they themselves were badly drunk and hence did not want to face a doctor at that odd hour. His stomach ache did not subside in the ensuing minutes. He then requested them to escort him to his residence.

His friends ultimately dumped him in their van and dropped him at a point, on a national highway, from where a taxi or an auto could be hired easily. Kanwar requested one of the duo to accompany him to his residence. Faced with a blank refusal, he was left with no alternative but to hire an auto rickshaw and head for his residence.

With great difficulty he managed to reach his residence and staggered straight up to his bedroom. It was well after two. He made a dash for his bed and went into deep sleep. After about an hour's sleep he got up, due to severe pain in his stomach as well as other parts of the body. However, he did not disturb any of his family members, despite his critical condition. In fact, his strong will power prevented him from seeking his family's assistance in going in for medical aid. Soon he rushed to the toilet and vomited about a bottle of blood, in one go. He felt awfully uneasy after vomiting blood but he preferred not to disturb any of his family members. I knew he was a man of extraordinarily strong will power. He, therefore, did not lose heart and washed down the blood, himself.

Amazingly, he somehow controlled himself and came staggering in front of the idols of Lord Krishna, goddess Durga and other deities, bowed before them and prayed from the core of his heart (with folded hands), for forgiveness and the sparing of his life. He vowed before the deities not to touch wine, or any intoxicant, for the rest of his life, once he was granted pardon. Thereafter, he came to the refrigerator staggeringly, took out milk and drank two full tumblers, in one go. After drinking the milk he retired to his bed. His uneasiness gradually started disappearing. Soon, he fell into a deep sleep. He woke up at about five in

the morning and felt better. His uneasiness had now, by and large, evaporated. He consumed about a quarter kilogram of refrigerated curd and again retired to his bed.

He finally woke up at about ten, feeling much better. He did not tell any of his kin about his having vomited blood, despite the fact that he was feeling very weak. He took complete rest the whole day and consumed only refrigerated milk, some curd and lemonade. In the evening, he went straight to the deities (the idols of gods and goddesses), bowed before them with folded hands and offered his repeated thanks to them, for according to him, a fresh lease of life. He kept offering obeisance to Him for quite some time, remorsefully and with tears in his eyes.

Days rolled by. He got up one fine morning in a state of perfectly normal health and decided to resume his business which had run into rough weather, because of the severe setback to his health. Strangely, he did not go in for any comprehensive medical treatment, or periodic check-ups, during his illness which was really grave.

The ensuing years saw him getting over his financial problems. He gradually cleared his debts and also managed to get back the pawned jewellery. He was a changed man now and could be seen progressing in his business affairs and heading towards prosperity. His spouse, aged mother and children, now had no complaint against him.

He had tremendous regard for his ageing mother. He was very particular about her health and needs. He had been fulfilling her each and every one of her desires. At one stage, he even took her on a pilgrimage, ensuring all possible comforts. He proved to be a very caring son.

The irony is that he could not rise to the expected level in his profession, probably because of some of his nature-born weaknesses and a few negative traits. His ego and lust for gold, were probably his two sworn enemies as far as my judgement goes. Another weakness in him was his superstitious nature. He would go on visiting fortune tellers, pandits (temple priests), astrologers, godmen etc. at short intervals, simply to get his problems remedied. He would not mind paying hefty *dakshinas* (offerings), to these people. He would keep himself engaged in the process of *upais* (remedial measures), suggested by the pandits, fortune-tellers, problem-solvers etc. I saw this man wasting a lot of money and time on these things. I often told him that the solutions to his problems did not lie in the hands of pandits etc. I had been, for many long years, telling him that the remedies for one's ills and problems lie only in one's own hands and with nobody else. I also used to tell him that many of his problems would automatically vanish, one by one, with the passage of time, provided he shunned his ego and lust for worldly glitter and also embraced virtues (the really good karmas). Another negative trait in him was his basic nature of overshadowing and overriding his fellow beings at times, simply for his personal gains. I had been, from time to time, advising him to overcome his negative traits (weaknesses), as a close friend but met with no success.

It will not be fair on my part if I fail to mention his positive traits also. He is a very good friend to his relatives and close acquaintances. 'A friend in need is a friend indeed', holds perfectly good in his case. Secondly, he has proved to be an extremely good host and is also compassionate towards the destitute and tormented souls. Thirdly, he is bestowed with an extremely good sense of humour. He can make people laugh at any time and in any situation. He has often spent money like water, on his family members and close acquaintances. But, to my mind, this is not a positive trait in him, as spending money lavishly on his kin, friends and on things of his liking, unnecessarily and going beyond his financial limits, is not wise. Even in the days of his financial crisis and constraints, he had been seen spending too much money, under one pretext or the other.

His decades-old habit of visiting pandits, astrologers,

palmists, fortune-tellers, living (so-called) godmen and godwomen frequently, with the sole aim of acquiring moveable and immovable assets and becoming rich, did not vanish. And then, he had been parting with hefty *dakshinas* to these living problem solvers all these years, almost blindly, forgetting that the solutions to his problems did not lie in their hands. Man, in fact, is himself the one who can remedy his problems by way of his karmas. If the karmas are good and aim at mitigating human sufferings, the problems automatically go on vanishing, one by one. Despite this hard truth, man, deluded by worldly glitter and materialism, prefers going to pandits, so-called godmen and godwomen, to seek *upais* (solutions, remedies), for overcoming his troubles as well as for becoming rich (irrespective of his good and bad karmas).

What can a pandit or fortune-teller (the so-called problem-solvers) do, if one's actions are not good? Miseries and problems emanate from one's deceitful acts (impure karmas). Don't think that one's bad karmas (deceitful acts harmful to the society and His scheme of things), will let one live peacefully. The divine, omnipotent, natural forces, won't let one go unpunished or unharmed, for one's deceitful dispositions. The forces will go on paying one back, in the same coin.

Chapter XVIII

Any person, at any time, can come to know about his or her level of placement in this world. For an on-the-spot self-assessment, what is needed is a little practice of concentrating the mind for a short duration, which is certainly not a difficult task.

The best place for introspection is one's dwelling and the best time is the relaxed moments of one's leisure hours.

Whenever you happen to find yourself relaxing comfortably, sitting on a sofa or an easy chair, just close your eyes and gradually make your brain criss-cross free. Feel as if your brain has become empty (of thought). Inculcate the feeling of nothingness.

Now with the placid mind, go in for introspection. Think about your life's journey. Flash your memories back to the stage-wise changes, right from your childhood to the moment you are undergoing introspection (via your adolescence, youth etc.), and sincerely try to get answers to these questions.

- How was your childhood—say, up to the age of ten? Did you have the basic amenities of good living? Were your parents caring ones and financially sound? Where did you receive your early education, in an ordinary school or a public school? Did you feel free, or in chains, in your childhood days? Were your parents polite, soft-spoken or loud, commanding and restricting? Did you always have a good pair of shoes, good clothes, good school uniforms and enough money to spend, on things of your liking? Do you feel your childhood was golden and full of cheer? Or was it cheerless, dull, devoid even of basic facilities? Was your house neat and tidy always? Or was it a small, dingy, stinking house, with dirty surroundings? Were you thrashed by your parents and teachers? Or was life smoothly sailing by? Did you ever have a grudge against your parents, for their frequent ill-treatment towards you? Do you feel your childhood, on the whole, was a happy one or was it troublesome?

- Now flash your memory back to your teens. Do you feel you were a happy-go-lucky child of your parents? Was it smooth sailing for you throughout your high school and college days? Did you have financial constraints, or were your parents in a position to spend lavishly on you? Were you really an intelligent student throughout, or just average? Did you like the environment around you? Was your parents' behaviour okay towards you? Were they rough quite often? Was it a memorable period full of joy, or was it cheerless, on the whole?
- After completing your education—did you have to struggle to stand on your feet? Did you step into the shoes of your father without having to make any effort? In other words are you a self-made man? Did you have a humble start and gradually rise to lofty heights? Or did your situation by and large remain as status-quo?
- What facilities and luxuries did you have, when you were a child and did your living standard go up, after entering into your profession? What difference do you find in your living standards at various stages - that is, childhood, adolescence, youth and as a married man, with dependants?
- Were you financially sound in the years or decades gone by, or are you financially sound now? Are you

ascending, or descending, at the moment?

- Do you feel you are still in need of more money and assets—moveable and immovable? How do you feel with your present lot? Are you contented with your present living standard and status, in the circle you move in?
- Were you satisfied then, or are you satisfied now? Do you take life as a struggle, or as a perennial adventure? Did you, at any stage, ever think that life was a burden and it was becoming more and more difficult to carry the burden? Are you satisfied with the environment you are living in?
- What about your surroundings? Is your dwelling place surrounded mostly by literate, or illiterate people? Do you have greenery and parks in the vicinity of your living place? Are the people around you reasonably good, in their behaviour, temperament, dialect, as well as good to the society around them? Do you feel you are compassionate to His creatures?
- What is the present trend of your life's journey? Are you climbing up or climbing down? Do you generally remain worried about maintaining your present living standard? Do you fear you won't be able to cope with the state of things in the coming times? What about your family environment? Have your dependants come up to your expectations or have they dashed your hopes to the ground? Are your family members cordial towards you and do you feel you are being served by your family members the way you deserve? Is your spouse an irritant by nature, or is she sweet in her temperament, with the people around her?
- Do you relish your food (including beverages, savouries and sweet things), to the last bite, or have

you been medically advised not to consume food which is to your taste?

- What about your contribution towards the society you live in? Have you been serving His creatures in sharing, or mitigating their miseries, in the active phase of your life? Does you simply care for your own bread and butter? What about your natural traits?
- Have you ever evaluated your positive and negative qualities? Do you possess, by your very nature, more positive traits than negative ones? Does the reverse hold true?
- Do you ever feel you receive punishment (in one form or the other), at times, by the natural forces, for your evil doings?
- Do you believe that the all-powerful, celestial forces commensurately react to a man's bad and good karmas?
- What is the trend of the liabilities and problems facing you? Have you ever thought of scaling down your ambitions?
- Do you believe in the natural phenomenon of attributing man's sufferings to his own bad karmas? Or do you take your sufferings to be predestined and inevitable?
- Have you remained, by and large, true to your profession (means of livelihood), or have you been adopting all sorts of unfair means to acquire riches?
- Do you, or your dependants, almost perennially remain in need of medical treatment? If so, have you ever sincerely given a thought to the root cause of this?
- Compare yourself to the people at large, the world over and try to get at how many are below and how many are above you, in comparison to your present

living standard.

In this way, keep on getting answers to all these questions and queries with a concentrated mind, absolutely free of biases.

This introspection will make you truly aware of your placement in this world. It will tell you how many people at large are above you and how many are below you, as far as your living standard is concerned. You will also come to know what is in store for you, in the approaching times; whether you will be a loser or a gainer. Your introspection will become your guiding force. Such periodical introspection will go on telling you your standing in this world and would also act as a pointer.

Making use of these pointers, you will be able to avert many unpleasant happenings, from time to time. It would tell you where you stand at any given moment.

Introspection can help you in rectifying your karmas and would thus keep you on the right track in life. It would make you aware of your shortcomings—which can be overcome one by one. These self-assessments are, truly speaking, blessings in disguise and your best friends.

Chapter XIX

Do you fear God? Why do you feel you are afraid of Him? A little introspection will make you visualise reasons behind your fear. He, if you sincerely acknowledge it, is one's best friend. He is kind to all His creatures.

He always remains close to those who perpetually long to remain close to Him, under all circumstances. Those who are afraid of Him are surely disillusioned souls. The hard fact is that most people fear Him because of their indulgence in sinful acts and evil-doings. Man becomes timid because of his vices and negative traits. The more he becomes harmful to His creatures, the more he inculcates His fear in himself.

If one starts shunning one's bad karmas (harmful acts), then the fear of God will start evaporating.

As a matter of fact, 'God-fearing' and 'fearing God' are altogether two different phenomena. In His scheme of things, amiable ones believe in remaining God-fearing, while those who perpetually fear God, are, by and large, sinful people, devoid of humility and compassion, unlike their God-fearing fellow beings.

The wise men whom we call God-fearing, are those who perpetually long to remain close to Him, in one way or the other, while those embracing materialism only, distance themselves from Him, during most of their life's spells.

He, undoubtedly, is kind to all His creatures, irrespective of whether they are animals, beasts or human beings. It depends upon the individual, whether or not he is capable of availing himself of His kindness.

Chapter XX

Differentiating between days of the week is just like committing a crime against His divine scheme. Wise are those who respectfully consider all the days to be alike and equally auspicious. All the days are good provided one is good. Unfortunately, people at large (mostly the illiterate and semi-literate and particularly womenfolk), are superstitious and blindly differentiate between days, out of sheer ignorance. One must have come across people who consider Tuesday the most auspicious day. Many observe fasts and do not eat onions and garlic on this day. Then there are people who are awfully afraid of Saturday (popularly known as 'Shani'). They do not buy, or sell steel items, particularly machines, motor cars, scooters or motor-cycles or even cycles, on this day. And there are people who give more weightage to Thursday. Most of them do not shave or get their hair cut, or wash their clothes, or hair, on this day.

The elite (highly educated, who go by logic), always consider all the days to be equal. They respect all the days and do not designate one above the other. If one is disrespectful to any particular day blindly, one is most likely to be ill treated by that day. So, one should be true to nature's automatic and flawless principles and stop differentiation. One should be logical and not be a mere blind follower.

Chapter XXI

As has been discussed in the foregoing pages, people at large adore countless gods, goddesses, deities, peers, saints etc., in their own ways and beliefs. It is not necessary that all such people are true worshippers of their gods.

Observing fasts, offering prayers to God (or the gods), on selected days only, bowing before the deities again and again, singing bhajans with the sole aim of pleasing them, (the gods, deities etc.), would be meaningless unless one is pure in one's thoughts and true to Him and His creatures. After all, one cannot bluff Him, by merely offering money, or installing His idols, in places of worship. What really counts is purity of mind and true devotion and certainly not just offerings and the installing of costly idols. In the affairs of temples and other places of worship, the majority of the worshippers unfortunately, are hypocrites. These poor souls can't understand that they are trying to bluff Him, instead of pleasing Him. Then there are people who, in the guise of religious persons and seemingly staunch devotees, devise ways and means of extracting profits and benefits for themselves. They go on with their malafide and deceitful activities for years and years, till they get cornered by the all-powerful, natural forces. Such people can be seen suffering from physical and mental ailments in the concluding scenes of their life's drama. They suffer intensely, as a result of their deceitful acts towards Him and His men.

Chapter XXII

The poet W H Davies has rightly said—'What is this life if full of care, we have no time to stand and stare?' Need I explain its meaning?

Anybody with a little inner vision can explore the secret of tension-free living. Unfortunately, there are quite a few people who can, in the true sense, make use of their inner vision to get at the truth. In the case of the majority of the people, materialism comes in their way. In many cases, people deluded by worldly glitter, keep on amassing wealth and acquiring more and more moveable and immovable assets, almost throughout their life. They hardly get any time to relish and enjoy the beauty of nature. They do not get time to pause and see the beauties of gracious nature around them. Their sole aim of living becomes accumulating more and more money—by fair means or foul. How can a person, perennially remaining involved in his worldly gains and physical comforts and setting aside all norms of a decent human being, be at mental peace? Peace is, after all, not a saleable commodity. One cannot purchase peace even by paying one's whole life's earnings. However, the hard fact is that getting peace (perfect tranquillity), does not cost anything. It is absolutely free, but for only those noble souls who, in the true sense, long for it.

Truly speaking, it is not that difficult to get real mental peace provided the determination is there. One must learn to compromise with the hard (and harsh), realities of life and one will soon be feeling one is heading towards tranquillity, inch by inch. One of the golden rules for attaining real mental peace is to learn the art of taking life as it comes. Learning to remain calm under all circumstances, acknowledging sincerely that one has come into this world against one's will and that one has been left with no alternative but to face the harsh realities of life. One is, after all, merely a puppet in the hands of destiny (the all-pervading omnipotent natural forces perennially encasing and limiting one's latitude and freedom), learning to get close to these gracious forces—seeking their help by surrendering oneself (from the core of one's heart), to them. Soon one will start feeling protected by these forces, to a considerable extent.

But to get close to these gracious and omnipotent forces is not an easy task. One will have to purify oneself inwardly and outwardly, by gradually getting rid of worldly blemishes, inculcating the natural qualities of a noble and kind human being. For killing the devils residing in one, it is necessary to stop hurting one's fellow beings. Have mercy on the helpless, hapless and those in distress. Help them. Help the destitute in mitigating their sufferings. Learn to remain aloof from the people embracing a demoniac nature. Don't curse a 'nature-cursed' living being. The process of getting purified (inwardly and outwardly), is certainly slow. It is time-consuming, very very gradual but certainly not beyond the control of a common human being. One's destiny perpetually goes on changing, in commensuration with one's moment-to-moment actions. One can, undoubtedly, attain purity of mind and actions slowly but surely, under all circumstances, even while remaining involved in all sorts of mandatory, worldly activities (of course, free from avoidable blemishes).

Thus, in this way, one will gradually start coming close to the all-powerful forces. The forces will also start taking care of one. The moment one starts feeling one's brain has become stable and remains unaffected by the hassles of physical existence, it is assuring and one has achieved one's goal. One will then certainly experience the unique taste of tension-free living (perfect tranquillity).

And now I shall be discussing those embodied souls who consider themselves self-sufficient and not dependent upon anybody, for their safeguard and physical protection. They probably do not believe in the existence of any natural force affecting their everyday activities. Nor do they seem to believe in the moment-to-moment change in their destiny, depending upon their good or bad karmas. They consider destiny, as a predestined thing, preordained by Him.

And if one is arrogant and considers oneself 'self-sufficient' and not dependent upon anybody for one's safeguard, one is awfully mistaken and is confining oneself to perpetual darkness, as all beings perennially remain dependent in one form or the other. Even after death, one is dependent upon one's kith and kin (and fellow beings), to carry the dead body to the cremation ground (or a graveyard or a cemetery).

And again, before one's birth one is helplessly dependent on one's mother who keeps one protected in her womb, for nine long months. Needless to say a man, perennially remains dependent upon something or the other, in one shape or the other, whether alive or dead. Can this great, universal truth, be denied or set aside?

Fools are they who (out of sheer ignorance), claim that they do not require anybody's assistance in protecting them. These so-called, self-dependent and self-reliant people, certainly are the children of pride. The poor embodied souls do not know that their physical existence is flawlessly dependent upon something (in countless ways), in a non-stop manner.

No one can survive independently in this mortal world, even for a moment.

Off The Track

He who does not love gold, is gold.

Chapter XXIII

One cannot get one's fate changed as per one's will, simply by chanting mantras, hearing sermons, bowing before deities, visiting *mazars* and *samadhies*, travelling to holy places, or seeking the blessings of modern godmen and godwomen and self-styled swamijis.

Nor can the pandits (temple priests), fortune-tellers, palmists, or astrologers, help one in any way to change one's fate to one's satisfaction and make one prosperous. What really counts is one's karmas (actions), alone.

Destiny, or fate, is never predestined or preordained. It is ever mutable, depending upon one's karmas. One's karmas alone, thus hold the key to one's fate. Wise men, thus, do not believe in a preordained or predestined fate.

It is pity that people at large, out of sheer ignorance, often curse their fate, while in trouble. One should not keep on cursing one's fate. It will keep on cursing one back, in a reciprocal manner. One is oneself the maker (or changer), of one's fate, by means of one's karmas alone.

Chapter XXIV

I shall now be penning down an incident which clearly suggests instant punishment to a criminal, by the all-powerful natural forces.

Somewhere in the mid eighties, I was travelling in a state transport bus in Haryana. My immediate co-traveller happened to be a middle-aged, educated lady, with an amazing all-round, cosmic knowledge. She soon fell into an interesting discussion with me about how sometimes the natural forces react (retaliate, so to say) instantly, to a diabolic offence. She narrated an incident wherein she was directly affected. I am delineating it below, in the first person. It goes like this—

'Some time back, I was travelling in a city transport bus in broad daylight. As the bus was nearing my destination, I left my seat and started moving towards the front exit. As the bus was slowing down, a young boy in his early twenties snatched my purse with a sudden jerk and swiftly headed to the exit and jumped down, while the bus was still in motion, giving me practically no time to react instantly. Soon I realised what had happened. I raised an alarm—"thief... thief... bag-snatcher... catch him... catch him..." This caught the attention of the bus passengers and a few bystanders. A stout young man swiftly went into action.

He started chasing the bag-snatcher without loss of a moment. As he was about to catch him, the thief took out a knife and brandished it, to discourage the chase. The chaser, undeterred by the snatcher's knife, kept on chasing him. The snatcher got confused and in a hurry, he threw the bag and ran across the road hurriedly to escape being caught by the undeterred chaser. As he jumped over the railing of the road divider, he fell flat on the carriageway and in the moment that followed, I saw him run over by a speeding vehicle. The young boy died instantly. I was completely shaken by this tragic incident. I felt deeply sorry about the young boy's instant death. I never wanted him to meet with such an abrupt end.'

The woman became silent for a few moments after narrating this incident. And then she spoke, 'From this unpleasant incident, we can infer that at times, crime and punishment take place almost simultaneously.'

After a brief lull, my co-traveller then started narrating another tragic incident which she claimed had happened, by and large, before her eyes. I am delineating this incident too, as precisely as it came out of her lips (of course, again in the first person)—

'During my Kanpur tenure, one of my distant acquaintances (a cousin, so to say), about ten years senior to me in age, happened to be a medium category industrialist running a couple of factories, with the assistance of about a couple of scores of workers, including a full-time manager. His only son, in his mid-twenties during those days, appeared to be a spoilt child. He had been married for two years and had fathered a beautiful, healthy, male child. We had been frequenting each other's residences on one pretext or the other. My cousin was certainly a multimillionaire (if I am not overestimating him), with gigantic, moveable and immovable assets. But he surely was proud, uncompassionate and full of vanity. And so was his only handsome young son, who was in the habit of slapping his father's factory workers on the slightest excuse and threatening others with his revolver. His proud father did not seem to discourage his son from thrashing the factory workers or showing his revolver to others, who slightly resisted his advances.

'One fine morning, he mercilessly thrashed one of the factory workers, a Garhwali boy in his early twenties, on the factory premises, simply on hearsay that he had stolen money from the pocket of one of his uncles. By chance, my only son (also in his early twenties during those days), happened to be there. He, too, on sheer hearsay, gave a couple of hard blows to the poor Garhwali boy, who started bleeding profusely. The poor boy, the only breadwinner for his widowed mother and a younger brother, repeatedly pleaded not guilty but his pleas fell on deaf ears. He was then pushed out of the factory premises by the factory owner's proud son. He went to his hut with his bleeding nose and injured limbs. His mother was deeply shocked to see her son's condition. She wept inconsolably for hours and hours. She cursed the factory owner's son severely. She did not eat and drink for three days and kept lying and weeping. However, the factory owner's son and my son were not even slightly sorry (or remorseful), for having mercilessly beaten the poor boy.

'A few days after the incident, the factory owner's proud and unremorseful son felt his right foot and hand going dead gradually. His parents, however, took it lightly and started giving him the medical treatment prescribed by their family physician. No improvement was noticed for many days. Despite the best medical treatment, the boy's condition started slipping from bad to worse. And in the days and weeks that followed, both the arms and the right leg of the boy, gradually went dead. His parents became extremely worried over their only son's rapidly deteriorating condition. They could now be seen running from pillar to post and leaving no stone unturned in getting the best possible medical treatment available on earth, for their son. They spent hundreds of thousands of rupees on the boy's treatment but to no avail. The boy's condition went on deteriorating at a fast pace. They had been shifting him from one hospital to another, from nursing home to nursing home, specialist to specialist, but were meeting with no success. And then they started offering prayers in temples, durgahs, mazars, shrines and other religious places of worship and also sought the blessings of pandits, faqirs, and *peers,* but all this proved futile. They had also been paying visits to the Garhwali boy's mother, asking for forgiveness. She did not forgive them. They offered a lot of money to her as well as incentives for her son, but all this had no effect on her. She told them that now even the gods could not reverse or neutralise a mother's curse. She at last suggested that they should stop meeting her any more as nullifying her curse had gone beyond her control.

'Then the inevitable happened. The young, handsome and only son of the multimillionaire parents died in the intensive care unit of a nursing home of national repute. The hard fact remains that even the ultramodern medical sciences could not withstand the onslaughts of a mother's curse. And the story does not end here,' the lady continued. 'My son too, who had given a couple of blows to the poor Garhwali worker without knowing the truth, had something going wrong with him within a few days of the day of the incident.

He complained of the development of a peculiar type of phobia in him, as well as occasional numbness of the hands and lips. He completely failed to spell out the nature of the phobia he was suffering from. He even stopped driving and paying proper attention to his business. He was shown to specialists and even to a psychiatrist, but there was no improvement. Almost all the mandatory medical tests were carried out, more than once. The doctor told me that all the limbs of the boy were functioning perfectly and that he did not have a blood pressure, or heart ailment either. The doctors and the psychiatrist advised him to feel totally relaxed and stop worrying about his business. They further advised him to watch comedies on TV, read interesting books and frequent cinema and other comedy shows. My son earnestly followed the advice of his doctors but there was no improvement. Ultimately, he had to be hospitalised for proper check-ups and treatment. He was kept in an air conditioned, private room, for five days and given the best possible medical care. The doctors told me that he was absolutely okay physically but, they could not find out the cause of the peculiar phobia in him. It was now about a month-and-a-half since my son had been able to devote time to his business. It took him about four months to get back to normal, but by that time he had severe setbacks in business. As per a rough assessment, the business setback and expenditure on medical treatment of my son cost us nearly a hundred thousand rupees. Obviously, the couple of blows given by my son to the poor, innocent son of a widow, proved very dear. I as well as other members of my family had to pass through a period of anxiety, stress and strain, many sleepless nights, besides a huge loss in business.

'But at the same time I saw nature's flawless justification behind our sufferings. The irony is, that the medical sciences (the specialists and psychiatrists), failed to diagnose the cause of the peculiar phobia. Nor could my son spell out the cause of his fear.'

The lady (my co-traveller) became silent for a few moments after narrating these unpleasant incidents and then these words came out of her mouth, 'To my mind, there is nothing more powerful on earth than a poor, hapless widowed mother's curse. So, beware of a mother's curse, the lady advised.

Chapter XXV

In the early sixties, one of my distant acquaintances came to my office one fine morning and asked me if I could lend him two hundred rupees, with the promise to return the same in a week's time. Because of my helpful nature, it did not take me much time to part with the two hundred rupees. The gentleman thanked me and disappeared in no time. He did not show his face for nearly three months. Then one day, he gave me a surprise by landing up in my office all of a sudden, not to return my money but to get some of his urgent, official business done, with my assistance.

I rendered him all the possible help he needed in getting things done, but certainly at the cost of my own work to some extent. He then got up, thanked me for my services and hurried to the exit. He looked back at me, gave me a smile and disappeared. However, he appeared again after three days in my office, to seek my advice (rather, my opinion), on an urgent official problem that had been confronting him for quite some time and which had taken an ugly shape by that time.

Again, my compassionate nature forced me to oblige him on the spot. Strangely enough, this time he regretted his inability to return my money. He, however, promised to return the money in a couple of days or so. I thought he had given the deadline and would stick to that. But this was not to be. He apparently failed to stick to his promised deadline. One day, a close friend of that gentleman came in contact with me, by chance, on some official business. Soon we became frank in our talks.

During our chit chat, I came to know that he (the man who had taken the loan from me), was not fair in his dealings and that he had bluffed others earlier, in the same fashion.

For a short while, I felt as if my helpful nature had betrayed me, as I too, had earlier been cheated more than once, almost in the same way. But I soon realised that the petty incidents of cheating did not effect or damage my straightforward, simple, helpful nature, in any way and I resolved to continue to stick to my very same nature

The fact remains, that in my case nature has been perpetually, at one time or the other, compensating me, with interest, for my losses, in peculiar but inexplicable ways—if I am not overestimating.

That man (debtor), did not meet me again, even after years had gone by. Many years later, I came to know from someone that he had suffered huge losses in business and was no longer in a position to repay his debts and loans. It further came to light that one of his daughters had been seriously ill for quite some time and was under expensive medical treatment and that the man was now leading a desperate life.

This piece of information about that man made me sympathetic towards him. Had he met me, I would have probably given him another two hundred rupees, in keeping with my compassionate nature. But the irony is that the gentleman never met me again.

Time, spanning several decades, saw me cheated by some of my close and distant acquaintances, in one form or the other. But after being cheated every time, I felt as if it was not I, but the cheats, who had been cheated in the true sense.

In my later years I have never seen a single cheat flourishing during any phase of his life. I have also seen some of them meeting with tragic ends. All the while, I have never in my life felt like deviating from my helpful and compassionate nature. The great nature (the omnipotent, omniscient, divine forces), have ever been compensating me handsomely, in unique but inexplicable ways, for my being cheated or defrauded by some of my malignant acquaintances and also strangers at times.

People at large, can be seen frequenting shrines, durgahs, mazars, or temples of innumerable devis and devatas as well as godmen and godwomen, with the sole aim of seeking either material gains and comforts or getting their mental and physical ills cured. But most of the people visit these places and also meet the so-called godmen and godwomen in the hope of becoming rich, by leaps and bounds or for getting their fate remedied to their advantage.

Of course, there are also those who visit these places simply for seeking the blessings of their gods. But their number is very small. The people frequenting their devis, devatas, peers, as well as present-day godmen, simply for their material gains, are comparable with the beggars with begging-bowls in their hands, collecting alms from door to door. Surely we all know that a beggar remains a beggar throughout his life. The alms he collects do not last long. In other words, his begging bowl, by and large, remains empty. It is the same in the case of men and women who frequent the places of their stone gods and live gods, begging for wealth, prosperity and physical comforts from them, ignoring their blemishes and damaging traits.

Undoubtedly they get from their gods what they desire but what they get (the alms), does not last long. The material gains, riches, etc. they get in their begging bowls (by entering into bargains with their so-called gods), vanish after some time. Their lust for wealth keeps on forcing them to go to their small and big lifeless gods, to beg. In this way, they become lifelong beggars, with begging-bowls—going from place to place, temple to temple, shrine to shrine, at short intervals, with the sole aim of collecting alms (material gains), from their gods.

Obviously, the professional beggars (with begging bowls in their hands) and the materialistic beggars frequenting the shrines and gods out of their unending lust for wealth, are one and the same thing. Both are beggars in one shape (or form), or the other.

Chapter XXVI

One of my acquaintances, Mohan (not his real name), once happened to be executing some petty, civil engineering work, under my official control and supervision, in the late eighties, in Delhi. He was thirty-four at that time and quite a smart and well-educated man. He was diabetic. Anyhow, one fine morning in winter when I was basking in the sun (taking time out of my awfully busy schedule to relax), and enjoying the pleasant and warm sun just in front of my office, he came to me, wished me and occupied a chair facing me. He, like many others around me (at that time), considered me a palmist and a fortune-teller. After exchanging the formal pleasantries, he stretched out his right hand towards me and requested me humbly, to tell him by scanning his palm what was in store for him in the days to come. He appeared, at that moment, to be somewhat dejected—probably because of his chronic ailments. Frankly speaking, I was never a sound palmist. Despite that, I decided to scan the lines of his palms. Earlier, the predictions I made in the case of a few of my close acquaintances amazingly, came out to be true to satisfying limits. And really speaking, I attributed those predictions to my spontaneous, intuitive power, bestowed on me by Him.

Mohan had for quite some time been surrounded by a number of problems (personal as well as domestic). One of his cardinal problems was his shattered health. He used to talk to me about his domestic problems and worries. He seemed awfully worried about his ageing parents, his school-going children, his spouse and a couple of other dependants. He apparently felt burdened by his mandatory, domestic liabilities, despite the fact that his financial position was not that bad. His kids (a son and a daughter), were receiving their education in a good public school. Of course, he owned a small but perfectly independent dwelling—the only plus point, as he often used to say.

Exposing his heart to me while I was scanning his lines, he told me he did not hope to live long and that he might collapse any moment. I, however, negated his utterance spontaneously by telling him he was not going to die so soon.

I examined his lines for a few minutes. I was taken aback to see his lifeline (with my limited knowledge but with a pinpointing, intuitive power), which indicated the abrupt end of his life at the age of around thirty-four plus.

Although I did not want to dishearten him by telling him that his life stood spent, my straightforward nature prompted me to make him aware of what his lines were indicating. He certainly seemed somewhat mentally disturbed after hearing from me about his approaching, dreaded moment. I, however, tactfully told him that my prediction might not come true, as sometimes one's will power overrides such predictions. He seemed relieved somewhat from his mental strain and anxiety on hearing this.

We then had tea and conversed about the progress of the work he had been executing. With my limited, but at times pinpointing intuitive power, I also told him that he would live a long life once he survived the predicted death; but all this was in His hands. 'Such miracles do happen,' I told him. He felt further relieved, on hearing these words from me.

A few minutes later, I asked him to accompany me to the site of the work under execution by him, to see the progress of a couple of petty but urgent jobs. Shortly, we both entered a gigantic hall, wherein Mohan's working team had been laying heavy-duty steel girders at a height of about twenty feet from the floor level.

As we looked up to see the progress of the girder laying, one of the girders (which probably lacked proper bearing at one end), came down with a thud, missing Mohan by a centimetre or so. I was at that time standing next to Mohan and was at a safe distance. Had the falling girder hit Mohan, it would have ended him, on the very spot. We both were stunned and shocked too, at the sudden fall of such a heavy iron—weighing quintals. It took Mohan quite a few moments to recover from the shock. It was certainly a great escape for both of us, from the jaws of death. The work came to a standstill. We came back to my office and tried to relax in our chairs. I ordered one of my men to bring water and tea.

And once again, my intuitive power prompted me to tell Mohan that he would now live a long life. A smile appeared on his face and I remember he kept thanking God for quite some time, for His blessing him, with a fresh lease of life.

Earlier too I had predicted that he would suffer from health problems of a serious nature as well as financial constraints at times, because of some of his negative traits as he was in the habit of making a fast buck, at the cost of his colleagues. I had also been warning him to shun the bad things in him, but there appeared to be no effect on him.

The fact remains that some of his negative traits, which were of a serious nature, did not let him rise to the heights of his expectations. Because he did not shun the bad traits, he had been embracing (probably because of his basic nature), the ensuing years saw him suffering from a series of setbacks in his business and health. There was a time when I had seen him rising to great heights in his profession, from a humble position.

He progressed in the beginning by leaps and bounds and

then, I also saw him climbing down from the lofty heights. I attributed his decline to his overstepping the natural barriers (the lakshman rekhas, so to say). He apparently did not bother about the reactions to his really bad actions—the deceitful ones.

The poor, embodied soul, probably did not believe in retaliation by the all-pervading and all-powerful divine forces to his bad-traited actions. And I had seen him paying a heavy price for his bad karmas, such as cunningly getting maximum work allotted, at the cost off his colleagues; making money by unfair means at someone's cost and maintaining double standards, always.

However, some changes in him were noticeable after he was granted a fresh lease of life (by Him). Many of his bad traits disappeared, with the passage of time.

A time came when I saw him flourishing once again. I noticed (with great interest), a lot of overall improvement in him, with the passage of time. He had been in touch with me for nearly a decade-and-a-half.

I last saw him leading a considerably good life—endowed with modern amenities, keeping normal health and appearing financially sound—certainly bent and broken (moulded), to a better shape, by the omnipotent, gracious forces, controlling us all.

Chapter XXVII

One of my close friends (also an engineer), who had been my classmate in the late fifties for three consecutive years, was once officially entrusted, in the mid-sixties with the work of widening the carriageway of a national highway, close to the outer limits of a metropolitan city. A petrol-vending-cum service station happened to exist at a safe distance from the existing edge of the stretch of national highway, earmarked for widening and was apparently not affected in any way. As the widening was in progress and was gradually nearing the petrol pump station, my engineer friend told the owner of the petrol pump to close it for about a fortnight, so as to enable him to take up the widening of the stretch facing it. The owner of the petrol pump politely told my friend that closing it for fifteen days at a stretch would adversely affect his business. But my engineer friend paid no heed to him and asked him to close the pump from the following Monday.

In a day's time the equipment and machinery, such as road rollers, paver, boiler, bitumen drums, etc. as well as the working gangmen reached the petrol pump station, to get ready to take up the widening of the stretch in front of it.

The engineer requested the owner to stop vending oil and other related servicing activities from the following day, so that they could carry out the widening, in front of the service station.

The gangmen in charge (on the engineer's instructions), displayed the caution board—'road closed... widening in progress... ' on both the approach roads of the service station as a result of which the vending of petrol, diesel etc.

automatically came to a standstill.

Although the owner of the petrol pump knew that the widening job is carried out piecemeal—not consecutively, and that the entire affected stretch in front of the petrol pump was not more than a three days' job, even then, he inwardly got prepared to oblige the engineer, in order to avoid confrontation and harassment.

The fact remains that the small affected stretch was not more than a couple of days' job and that, too, to be done on different days. In fact, there was no need to get the service station closed at all.

It took the petrol pump owner no time to guess what the engineer's intention was. He invited him to his cabin, on the pretext of having tea with him. While they were sipping tea, he took out a few hundred-rupee notes from his table drawer and handed them over to the engineer. The engineer counted the money and told the owner to part with some more money. The owner thus had to shell out the remaining hundred-rupee notes, to satisfy the engineer.

Interestingly, the petrol pump station had to be closed for two nights only and that, too, on different days.

I came to know about all this—the way my engineer friend had blackmailed the owner of the service station—from one of my acquaintances who, by chance, during the road-widening operation, had visited that petrol pump to get his vehicle serviced and who, during his chit-chat with the owner came to know even the exact amount the engineer got from him, out of undue gratification.

Later, my engineer friend admitted to me that he had to play this trick to extract money from the service station owner. I told him it was not at all fair on his part to extract money like that and that it amounted to sheer blackmail. At this, my friend retorted that everybody was indulging in such tactics and tricks those days, to supplement their income and that he was no exception. He even advised me to make use of such tactics to extract money from the affected people and contractors. I strongly reacted to what he uttered and disapproved of his malicious designs of making quick bucks. I advised him to stop blackmailing people and to desist from adopting corrupt ways of making money, lest he should regret it one day. But all this had no effect on him. Rather, he expressed his satisfaction on having received a bribe from the service station owner.

He became more and more corrupt, with the passage of time. He had been using all sorts of ugly and malicious tricks, to make more and more money. A stage then came, when he came to be considered by his colleagues and acquaintances as one of the most corrupt engineers. The ill-gotten money later proved to be an instrument of destruction for him. Gradually he became an alcoholic and a chain-smoker. He also started visiting cabaret shows, brothels and gambling dens. He was apparently doing all these bad things at the cost of his dependants. I had been making attempts, at times, to convince him that he was heading towards a point of no return, at a breakneck speed. However, I failed in all my attempts. Once he even asked me to mind my own business.

He was spending a major chunk of his money on himself, drinking, smoking, gambling and womanising, while his dependants felt undernourished, uncared for and totally neglected.

The years rolled by and a time came when this man, who once possessed robust health, now looked old, exhausted and infested with serious diseases. Money flowed like water on his medical treatment. The irony is that his shattered health did not deter him from his awful drinking and awful smoking habits. He could no longer work in the field now and as such, was given desk duty (devoid of chances of any extra income or gratification), on compassionate grounds. Gradually he became so weak that he started taking leave of all kinds. And after exhausting the annual quota of his leave, he even used to avail himself of leave on half pay and leave without pay etc. This continued for some years.

With the passage of a few more years, he could now not even walk properly—and ultimately became bedridden. And thus compelled by circumstances, he had to seek voluntary retirement at a time when his superannuation was at least five years away. This premature retirement badly shattered his domestic setup. His spouse became a heart patient; his only son emerged as a notorious young boy, with all the bad habits and his two daughters, who had completed their graduation creditably had come of marriageable age.

When I met him last, he was confined to bed. He was too weak to get up on his own. However, he boldly admitted to me that he was suffering intensely because of his bad karmas—and that he felt completely cornered by the great nature.

The huge sums of money he had made, by all sorts of unfair means, ultimately became an instrument of destruction for him.

Chapter XXVIII

If one is not fair to His creatures, one should not expect Him to be fair to one. If one is cunning, be assured, He is more cunning. And if one is an egoist, be assured, He will crush one's ego some day.

And if one is trying to become rich and prosperous by corrupt means, at the cost of His people, be assured, one is a bad bargainer and also a bad businessman.

The bucks that come quickly also go quickly.

If one considers oneself a big cheat, be assured, He is a master cheat. If one cheats His men, He won't spare one. If one has been fraudulent and deceitful—He won't, ultimately, let one go scot-free.

I have not hitherto come across, or heard about an evildoer who has led a peaceful life, in the last run.

Criminals and evildoers, as per a natural rule, do not survive for long. Their lives are always short. They may appear to be flourishing some time, but they surely meet with tragic ends—generally in the prime of their lives. Then, so long as they live, they keep on running and stumbling over natural hurdles and barriers. The ever-chasing, omnipotent natural forces, do not let them remain at peace, till their doomsday.

Deceitful people, too, cannot lead a peaceful life. The forces keep on retaliating against their deceitful advances and frustrate them ultimately.

The fact remains that the evildoers cannot escape punishment at the hands of the all-powerful and all-pervading, celestial forces. The forces punish them in commensuration with their crimes.

And, this is what the ever-true theory of crime and punishment is. Nature perennially maintains the balance of crime and punishment in peculiar, but inexplicable ways.

Chapter XXIX

The great natural forces punish us and reward us depending upon our good and bad karmas commensurately, at the most appropriate times, in countless ways. They make us suffer physically or mentally, for our rebellion against His scheme of things.

One must have come across people perpetually suffering from mental pains (agonies), or physical disabilities, for no apparent reason. But certainly the reasons behind one's physical or mental sufferings are always there. An average human being finds no major reason behind an embodied soul's sufferings. Even the sufferer, at times, fails to find any reason, or justification, behind his pains.

However, the bitter truth is that one's sufferings and pains cannot be devoid of a valid reason. Similarly, one's blissful, tranquillising spells or moments, too, are not devoid of flawlessly valid reasons.

We often see people – generally wealthy and affluent – deprived of certain privileges, otherwise absolutely essential, towards an interesting and enjoyable physical life. Again it seems, all this is for no apparent reason.

Why can't most people get at the root cause or causes of their pain? Obviously we, the embodied souls – made of flesh and blood – are spiritually too weak to comprehend the upkeep of the nature-made, most authentic, irreversible, divine equilibrium, of crime and punishment. We thus suffer for our misadventures against nature. And we also, at times, experience ecstatic moments and spells—apparently because of pure actions (good karmas).

There are in this world a large number of wealthy and

affluent people, who are medically forbidden the use of some of the truly relishing ingredients of food, such as sugar, salt, fats, fried eatables, spiced food, juice containing a high percentage of sugar, even rice, milk and milk products etc. Some of them are made to live their whole life on saltless, sugarless, fatless—in other words tasteless, ingredients. They apparently can't enjoy their lives in the strict sense. The great nature won't let them relish tasty food, despite their enormous wealth. Of what use is their wealth and riches if they have been forbidden, forever from relishing physical pleasures?

Most of them can be seen, by and large, perpetually under expensive medical treatment. Instead of relishing tasty food, the forces, under His supreme command, make them eat bitter and tasteless medicines.

There are those rich people who lack an appetite for food, for no apparent reason. Their enormous wealth cannot restore their appetite in a natural, lasting way. They perennially remain dependent on expensive medicines. In other words, expensive medical care, keeps them alive. They also lack peace of mind, because of the serious nature of their ailments. Obviously, their vast wealth and riches fail them, when it comes to leading a comfortable and peaceful life.

One cannot, after all, buy ecstasy and eternal peace even with one's entire wealth. Of course, there are those rich men, too, who enjoy a blissful life (by and large) and many of them remain disease-free to a considerable extent, even till their later days. In such cases, nature has a justification behind their rapture. In His eyes, this category of rich people deserve the fruit of their riches on account of a number of factors—not visible to the naked eye—and also incomprehensible to the commoners.

We can undoubtedly, buy some physical comforts with our money, for some time. But certainly we cannot purchase nature's blessings, even with our entire wealth.

And one must have observed in one's everyday life, people who are poor but are perfectly hale and hearty and can be seen relishing every bit of whatever food they can afford.

They, unlike their rich fellow human beings, are not forbidden any of the delectable ingredients of food. Nor do they suffer from any serious ailment (in most of the cases). They do not have to spend much money on their day-to-day physical problems. They generally get cured of their ailments on the state's expense, as they do not go in for costly treatment, unlike their rich brethren.

But this does not mean that all rich people suffer because of their ego of being rich, or their callousness (towards the poor probably), and that all the poor and the commoners do not suffer. Both suffer alike, in one way or the other. No one can escape sufferings in this mortal world. As per His scheme of things, sufferings and ecstasy go side by side. And the fact remains that there are generally more sufferings in store, than ecstatic spells in the life of each and every embodied soul that has come in this world—irrespective of its placement (living status or standard, so to say).

But the hard fact also remains that rich men, in general, lead more desperate lives, as compared to their poor fellow beings. The commoners (between the rich and the poor), are comparatively a satisfied lot.

However, no one on earth can escape sufferings, be they rich, poor or commoners. This is what the divine scheme of things is.

Our karmas undoubtedly, become the cause of our joys and sorrows, ecstasy and pain.

An embodied soul's greatest treasure is its perennial good health—devoid of any major ailment. A rich man's entire wealth cannot match this treasure of nature.

Obviously, all beings have not been entitled (by Him),

to sound health. A sound physique is nature's greatest gift and a blessing that is not bestowed on all. Man's karmas are his key to disease-free living.

The ever-chasing, omnipotent forces, spare none for one's misadventures against mother nature.

Chapter XXX

At times, I have often felt as if I have been celestially gifted, to explore the secrets of nature and to get at the flawless universal truth.

Despite my limited, inner vision and worldly knowledge, my experimentation with some people close to me, in the decades gone by, have enabled me to come out with some amazing inferences.

I studied the people (mostly my close acquaintances and relatives), with regard to their behaviour towards their fellow beings and their contribution to the world. I found that those who had been breaking nature-born conventions, transgressing all limits and treating nature disrespectfully, were seen suffering mentally as well as physically, in the last run. Time saw them being confronted with nature-born impediments at most of the time in their lives. I did not see them living a comfortable and trouble-free life. I never saw them at peace. The fact remains that they had been hostile in their attitude towards nature and nature had been hostile to them, in unique ways. Blinded by materialism and worldly glitter, they had been flouting natural conventions and laws and overstepping the lakshman rekhas and nature had been paying them back in the same coin, intermittently.

Those who had been rude in their temperament towards their fellow beings and indulged in activities harmful to living beings and nature's treasure, were ultimately (though gradually), cornered by the natural omnipotent forces—and met with disastrous ends, in the last run. Nature cornered them for their misadventures and evildoings—the bad karmas—and inculcated in them the feeling of helplessness, in the evening of their lives.

Interestingly, in the concluding phase of their lives' dramas, most of the extreme sufferers, unhesitantly admitted that their immense sufferings and cornerings were attributable to their misadventures and hostile attitude towards nature and that all their riches and muscle-men could not extricate them from the clutches of the ever-chasing and all-powerful, natural forces.

And I also came across those (small in number, of course) who had been, by their very nature, compassionate towards living, embodied souls, highly respectful to nature, virtuous and above all, God-fearing (in the true sense) and who ultimately came out victorious. I saw many of them leading peaceful and disease-free lives, in their concluding years.

My experiments revealed to me that the noble and virtuous – the harmless and compassionate creatures of God – stood the test of time. Whenever they were confronted with troubles or physical problems, the gracious, all-pervading and all-powerful forces, came to their rescue, in unique but inexplicable ways. On the whole, I saw them sailing smoothly in their lifeboats, even on turbulent waters. I saw some of the evildoers consistently receiving punishment, at the hands of natural forces, for their bad karmas. Their wealth and muscle power could not protect them from the punishment they had been getting intermittently, at the hands of the omnipotent forces.

My experiments also revealed that the equilibrium of crime and punishment is consistently and flawlessly upheld, by the great natural forces, in countless but inexplicable ways.

In my laboratory (confined of course to my physical existence), I came across almost all kinds of people—the good ones and the bad ones, partly good and partly bad ones, the virtuous, the diabolical, the cruel, the compassionate, the clever, the cunning, the sober, the God-fearing—and the people with virtues and vices of extreme nature. I became sure about one thing—and that is that I did not come across a single person whom I could designate, or label, as a 'perfectly virtuous', or a 'perfectly diabolic' person. An average being, as we all know, is after all a blend of virtues and vices; positive and negative traits. Nobody is perfect, or free from blemishes, in this mortal world. However, in our physical existence, there are two distinct categories of people—the virtuous ones and the evil (the wrongdoers, so to say). Both are punished and rewarded intermittently, in commensuration with their bad and good karmas.

The embodied soul thus, is himself the largest source of his sorrows and joys, depending upon his actions—the karmas.

Natural forces, being all-pervading and all-powerful, are the embodied soul's greatest protectors. They meticulously strike in unique ways—invisible to the human eye, at the most appropriate time and avert disasters. These all-pervasive and all-powerful, gracious forces, would stand by one (provided one deserves it), in one's desperate hours.

Take care of the natural forces, and the forces will take care of you—what I mean is that if one would respect these gracious forces, by not transgressing their limits and barriers, they would reciprocate and stand by one, at the time of one's need. Honour the forces, and the forces will honour you. Respect the night (which is meant for rest and sleep), and the night will respect you. It will keep you mentally and physically fit. Take care of your physique, and your physique (sound body), will take care of you. Surrender yourself to the supreme power (commanding the forces), and the supreme power will surrender itself to you—that is, it will provide you full protection from all worldly ills. Help living beings in distress, and their blessings will help you in crossing the ocean of your life smoothly (even on turbulent waters). Adore Him, He will adore you. Come under His supreme command and He will come under your command. Respect the environment and the environment will respect you—it will make you a blessed man and spiritually sound.

Respect the food you get to eat and the food would respect you—that is, you will relish its each and every bite, till your doomsday. Bow before the supreme power (as a disinterested and selfless creature), and the power will bow to you i.e. It will be at your command.

And, if you abandon Him, He will abandon you. If you keep on cursing your fate, your fate will keep on cursing you. If you stop taking interest in your life, your life will also stop taking interest in you.

Apparently all these things—the natural phenomena, are based on one of the basic principles of Divine Nature's give and take principle.

This principle holds good in our everyday life. In fact, the entire existence of the embodied souls on earth is based on this golden principle of nature. The natural forces (under His supreme command), ensure the perennial upkeep of this principle.

So if one is immensely close to the beauties of nature, such as lush green forests, meadows, snow-clad cliffs, mountains, valleys, oceans, the sunrise, the sunset, bright starry nights, moonlit nights, limitless vast space, cloudy skies, rainfall, snowfall, appearance of a spectrum, misty and hazy panoramas, sweet, music-producing rivers and streams, morning mists, lakes, surrounded by green mounds, sudden appearance of jet black clouds, cold, bright, sunny wintry days, uneven green landscapes etc.—the beauties of nature will also remain close to one—giving one everlasting ecstasy.

Man, in fact, is naturally bestowed with spiritual powers with which he can (if he sincerely wishes to), explore the secrets of nature. He can explore the inner, divine power, to such an extent that he can attain perfection to the level of his supreme Lord.

People the world over worship innumerable gods and goddesses in their own ways. There is no dearth of religions and faiths either. But the wise are those who staunchly believe in the existence of the one and only God. Such people worship Him from the core of their hearts, disinterestedly and selflessly. They never demand anything (like physical comforts and gains), from Him, while offering their prayers. They do not enter into any bargain with Him. They perennially remain satisfied at heart. These are the people who can be designated as the true worshippers of God. They pray simply for their liberation from the shackles of births and deaths and for universal peace. Of course, such embodied souls are rare and indeed adorable. They, in fact, are no less than living gods. The supreme power (God), undoubtedly, stands by them perpetually and looks after the mandatory requirements of their everyday life. They are the real gainers.

The irony is that most people all over the world worship their innumerable gods and goddesses and even living godmen and godwomen, with the sole aim of amassing more and more moveable and immovable assets, simply to ensure for them and their dependants, all the worldly comforts and riches. They worship him simply for their material gains—in a selfish way. They try to please them (their gods), by offering money and hefty donations. They often enter into bargains with Him in countless manners, simply for their personal gains. Such people are the real losers.

Real worshippers, unlike their greedy and materialistic fellow beings, do not get carried away by conflicting statements about the absolute power. They remain ever firm in their belief, under all circumstances, in the existence of the one God only, governing the universe, in the form of celestial forces, omnipresently existing and flawlessly discharging their assigned functions—visible to the rare, embodied souls who are bestowed with the third eye.

These all-pervading celestial forces, under His supreme command and control, keep the truly virtuous souls protected from all the worldly ills and blemishes, emanating from greed, anger and ego.

Off the track

Don't alienate Him; nor get alienated from Him. In both eventualities, you surely stand doomed and cease to be a human being.

Chapter XXXI

When I finally retire to my bed, after the day's hassles and tiring activities, I feel as if I am standing as a convict before a jury—the divine, unseen, Supreme Power, clearing my position on the charges levelled against me. The argument between me and the jury goes on for quite some time. At times, I have been held guilty and punished. But during most of these trials (in the divine court), I plead not guilty and have often been acquitted.

Off the track

Neither is He great without His true adorers, nor are His adorers great, without Him.

Chapter XXXII

Portraits of persons who have remained close to me, for decades—

1 One of my God-given relatives—a man senior to me in age by many years, was in the habit of humiliating his acquaintances and relatives around him, on the slightest pretext. To my mind, his habit of slandering and humiliating the humble, simple embodied souls during functions, get-togethers and religious ceremonies, was by virtue of his very basic nature. He had many positive traits too, but this highly negative trait of humiliating the humble and poor, was conspicuous. His greatest weakness was his better financial background and official status. Despite his negative traits, he always considered himself to be helpful and generous. His acquaintances knew well that he was simply a hypocrite. His other sworn enemies were his egoism, pride and cleverness. He was, so to say, a man who slaps a man according to his rank. He did not desist from inflicting mental injuries on his near and dear ones. I, too, have often been slandered by him at functions, get-togethers simply because I was financially weak and not as affluent as he was.

For decades I had been tolerating silently humiliation and insults at his hands, like so many others—simply because he was my God-given relative and senior to me in age and status.

'God has given you relatives; thank God you can choose your friends,' has very rightly been said by someone.

I often heard persons who had been facing humiliation at his hands showering curses on him. The decades rolled by, but his habit of slandering, humiliating, insulting and even letting people down, did not recede.

I also observed that the great nature had been punishing him intermittently, in unique ways, but he did not appear to realise this. I saw him sometimes suffering from a series of setbacks. But this did not deter him in any way, from using indecent utterances and hurting words for his relatives and acquaintances.

In the concluding phase of his life, time saw him bent and broken to a better shape. The command he enjoyed in his active life because of his official position, had vanished. There was no one left to hear his commands and orders. Besides, he was now suffering from a number of ailments and mental worries.

At times, he had been receiving severe jolts at the hands of the omnipotent forces—ranging from incurable ailments, to tragedies of his dear ones.

A day came when he was completely shaken, as if he was back to square one. From his talk he now appeared to be desperate and considered life meaningless and a burden. I am sure his ego and anger, which he had had at one stage, had by and large subsided. He had probably alienated himself from everyone, by slandering and insulting his relatives and acquaintances. He had lost confidence in himself. He had probably realised that his sufferings were the outcome of his bad behaviour towards his humble, poor, simple-hearted relatives and of the curses they had been showering on him, from time to time. But it was too late now, for him to repent.

II Now I shall be delineating the portrait of a lady.

She is like a person who lives in a glass house but is not afraid of throwing stones at others. She is:

A person who never finds any fault in herself but finds faults with her relatives and acquaintances around her.

A person who has yet to appreciate any of her relatives, or an acquaintance.

A person who claims to be close to her gods and goddesses and even live godmen and godwomen, but in fact, is simply a hypocrite and an egoist.

A person who, by her very nature, is suppressing, harsh and cruel, but claims to be compassionate towards the poor, oppressed, destitute and downtrodden members of society.

A person who is a destroyer of food articles, such as fruit, vegetables, bread and countless other articles, including medicines—a waster of eatables.

A person who is a destroyer of domestic peace.

A person who would willingly contribute, in terms of money and articles towards community kitchens (langars on auspicious occasions) and *havans* and would also pay hefty dakshinas to the priests and false saints and so-called godmen, but would not offer a penny to a genuinely, needy soul.

A person who would devote hours and hours daily, on pleasing her stone and live gods, by reciting bhajans and chanting mantras and attending community kirtans, instead of keeping her household in order.

A person who finds happiness in offering delicious food and fruit etc. to the temple priests, so-called swamis and gurus, but may not necessarily offer these delicious dishes (halva, kheer etc), to her spouse.

A person who is highly stubborn, daring and relentless and would not let anybody get the better of her, in arguments and even scuffles.

A person who is too shrewd and witty to let anybody overpower her, in a war of words.

A person who will never keep her house, particularly her kitchen, neat and tidy.

A person who is a great listener to the discourses of so-called godmen and godwomen, at different venues and at different times.

A person who, at times, may not stick to her word.

A person who is a great worshipper of countless deities, in their numerous forms.

A person who has seldom been seen extending a helping hand (in the true sense), to truly deserving persons in distress.

A person who often changes her statements.

A person who will appreciate anybody, for his rendering useful services and advice of course, with the exception of a few of her near and dear ones, who may have risen to lofty heights, by embracing corrupt means. She appreciated these few who in their lifetime, made a quick buck by unfair means, rather than hard work.

A person who often criticised her spouse for not raising huge bank balances and acquiring moveable and immovable assets.

A person who has never been found to be satisfied with her lot.

A person who would keep on cursing her near and dear ones—particularly her spouse—on one pretext or the other.

A person who has perpetually remained and would continue to remain, in a commanding position.

A person who forces her family members to adore the gods and goddesses and deities the way she does—almost like a dictator.

A person who has never learnt to eat humble pie.

A person who behaves ruthlessly with humble and poor fellow beings.'

A person who surely is mentally sick, but will not

admit that she is so.

A person whose harsh words and utterances make a number of her near and dear ones vanish from her life, gradually. She makes her friends her foes with the passage of time.

A person who has been visiting places of worship and listening to the discourses of so called high-profile godmen and godwomen and also reciting verses from the religious texts (Bhagavad-Gita, Ramayana, Puranas etc.), for many long years, but all this has had no effect on her behaviour and attitude. She continues to be harsh and humiliating towards most of her fellow beings.

Her daily poojas (prayers), which last for hours and which have been going on for decades together, which failed to overcome her bad traits, such as hypocrisy, ego, anger and greed.

A person who creates problems for her own family members, because of her rigid stand.

A person who remains stuck where she had been, decades back. Bhakti and Pooja have had no effect on her in any way.

A person who suffers a series of set backs in her health in her advanced age, probably because of her failure to overcome her mighty enemies viz.—hypocrisy, ego, anger and greed (for more and more wealth and assets).

It would, however, not be fair on my part, if I failed to portray some of her positive traits too. She has been—

- A nourishing and highly caring mother.
- An excellent cook (at times).
- An excellent hostess (at times).
- A protector of her family members in a unique manner, depending upon the warranting situation.
- A panacea for some persons around her.

- A storehouse of bhajans, sacred verses, 'shlokas', myths (kathas), and of course, old memories.
- A person who claims to be close to her deities with the blessings of whom she can cure anyone's chronic diseases and can get any intricate problem solved.
- A person who will always follow her own logic, at her whims and fancies and will not like to entertain any argument from any quarter.
- A person who, at times, appears sober and mentally stable
- A person who will leave no stone unturned in solving others' problems but fails to find solutions to her own domestic problems.
- A person who blindly (or shall I say staunchly?), believes in myths and narrations (incidents and stories), contained in the Hindu religious scriptures. She will not entertain any debate, or argument, regarding the authenticity of narration and myths.

Chapter XXXIII

I saw some of my close contemporaries of the late fifties and sixties who had been ignoring natural barriers, celestial signals and warnings, flouting every convention, breaking laws set by Mother Nature and transgressing all limits, suffering intensely later, from numerous physical problems and mental agonies, in one form or the other. To my mind, they were reaping the crop (of karmas), they had sown at one time, out of sheer ignorance.

I also saw those (of course, small in number), who had been respecting (in the true sense), the natural barriers and conventions and making no attempt to overstep the lakshman rekhas or transgress natural limits—later sailing smoothly in their lifeboats, even through turbulent waters. They were seen sailing smoothly—almost disease-free and free of any major problem – in a beautiful environment. Their children and grandchildren came up to their expectations. I saw them bowing before the all-pervading omnipotent forces (under his supreme command), and I also saw the (forces) protecting them, from worldly blemishes and ills, in amazing ways and means.

My nature-born zest, kept me monitoring my contemporaries (of the fifties and sixties), closely regarding their behaviour towards Mother Nature and the living beings around them. I studied their performance and contributions to the world—spanning several decades. What I have delineated in the foregoing paragraphs and pages regarding them (my contemporaries), is the harsh truth.

The forces had been retaliating in a befitting manner, their misadventures and onslaughts against Mother Nature.

None of them was allowed to go scot-free. They were punished for their crime against the Divine setup. None was exonerated for his or her onslaughts, against His scheme of things.

At least a couple of my contemporaries of the early sixties who had been arrogant because of their riches, muscle power and connections with high-ups (top brass) and also cruel and rude in their temperament towards their fellow beings, were later seen to be completely overshadowed and cornered by the Supreme Power, in inexplicable unique ways. They could not extricate themselves from the clutches of the celestial, omnipresent and omnipotent, mysterious forces.

Chapter XXXIV

Man comes into this world (against his will, as we all know), and vanishes from the scene, after passing through various stages of life—from infancy to dotage.

During his life's non-stop journey, he is constantly monitored and chased by the Supreme Power (the invisible, all-pervading, omnipotent divine forces), for his moment-to-moment actions and contribution to the divine nature.

He is rewarded and punished intermittently, for his good and bad karmas.

He undergoes pleasures and pains, joys and sorrows, helplessly.

But surely, it seems apparent, that those who break laws set by nature, flout divine conventions, overstep natural barriers and transgress all limits, are not reborn as human beings.